Praise for *Forward*

"With so many suffocating in pessimism today this book is a breath of fresh air that provides the life-giving, biblical optimism we need to overcome our current challenges and create a better tomorrow. Dr. David Jeremiah provides us with oxygen for our souls and points us *Forward* with a plan to live the life God has created us to live. I'm so thankful for him, his ministry, and this great book that I'll be sharing with everyone I know."

—JON GORDON
BESTSELLING AUTHOR OF *THE ENERGY BUS* AND
THE POWER OF POSITIVE LEADERSHIP

"From the first page of the introduction in this book a fresh flame of hope and purpose was ignited in my heart. If, like me, you have felt discouraged, disappointed, or unsure about what lies ahead in this season, Dr. Jeremiah walks us forward with practical steps and profound biblical wisdom. Forward, always forward! This is an important book!"

—SHEILA WALSH
AUTHOR AND SPEAKER
CO-HOST OF THE *LIFE TODAY* TELEVISION PROGRAM

"In Dr. David Jeremiah's new book *Forward*, we are encouraged and guided to find God's perfect will for our lives and for our tomorrows. In this time of seemingly little hope he lets us know with Christ all things are possible."

—DAVID GREEN
FOUNDER AND CEO, HOBBY LOBBY

"Fear arises when our personal worlds spin out of control or the future seems uncertain. At such times we look for voices of calm and reason. Voices like David Jeremiah's are a trustworthy source of clarity and understanding. What better time than today for his new book, *Forward*, an encouraging reminder of God's guidance and sovereignty."

—MAX LUCADO
PASTOR AND BESTSELLING AUTHOR

"Personal. Practical. Powerful. That's the best way to describe the dynamic message in Dr. David Jeremiah's timely and terrific book *Forward: Discovering God's Presence and Purpose in Your Tomorrow*. Each chapter is a step-by-step guide to living out the dreams God has planted in us. I've read many books that told me God *wanted* to do great things in my life, but this one tells me *how* to be on His track to actually experience it. Read it for yourself, give it to family and friends, and follow its solid biblical blueprint for living and leaving this life with a legacy."

—MIKE HUCKABEE
FORMER ARKANSAS GOVERNOR
HOST OF THE *HUCKABEE TALK SHOW*

"From dream to deliverance, Dr. Jeremiah gives practical principles for life's march forward by daring us to have and pursue a dream. Knowing that no dream can live without hope, he urges us to embrace what is eternal by investing our passions in ways that make it possible for us to outlive our lives with tomorrow always unfolding 'at the speed of grace.' What a thought! What a goal! What a trajectory to the most lasting of dreams-come-true! Yes, forward, indeed!"

—BILL AND GLORIA GAITHER

"I have read every book David Jeremiah has written, but none have impacted me like his most recent, *Forward*! I measure a book by how much marking I do and how many pages I have folded down—and I've done a ton of both with this book! I couldn't put it down; I read this book in one sitting, and I won't be surprised if you do too."

—PAT WILLIAMS
NBA EXECUTIVE AND HALL OF FAMER
AUTHOR OF *REVOLUTIONARY LEADERSHIP*

"The shortest verse in the Bible where Jesus is speaking is Luke 17:32. In it He said, 'Remember Lot's wife.' But don't let the concise nature of those three words fool you. They pack a punch. It's easy to become salty—held hostage by your yesterday and kept from experiencing the blessings God has for your tomorrow. In his new book *Forward* Dr. David Jeremiah will help you cut and run, dropping the things weighing you down so you can face the future full-throttle."

—LEVI LUSKO
PASTOR, FRESH LIFE CHURCH
AUTHOR OF *TAKE BACK YOUR LIFE*

"If there was ever a time to focus on your dream, and move *Forward* . . . it's *now*! This book is guaranteed to get your mind right . . . and get your soul right too. If you are looking to ignite your passion, deepen your purpose, and create more impact, read this book . . . it will change your life!"

—TODD DURKIN, MA, CSCS
OWNER, FITNESS QUEST 10
AUTHOR OF *GET YOUR MIND RIGHT*
HOST OF THE *TODD DURKIN IMPACT SHOW PODCAST*

"Dr. Jeremiah beautifully teaches the liberating lesson of letting go of our past and pressing *Forward* with the perfect plan God has for each of us. I plan to borrow (with credit) his eloquent observation that with the Lord 'our future is always unfolding at the speed of grace!' A positive, uplifting, and motivating read for every believer."

—MATTHEW CROUCH
PRESIDENT, TRINITHY BROADCASTING NETWORK

"Using a mosaic of real-life stories along with practical steps that motivate and direct readers to go *Forward*, David Jeremiah propels believers out of complacency into a life of fulfillment and purpose. I recommend this easy-to-read, easy-to-understand, encouraging, and practical book for all followers of Jesus."

—ANNE GRAHAM LOTZ
INTERNATIONAL BIBLE TEACHER
AUTHOR OF *JESUS IN ME*

"It doesn't matter if you are leading your family, your business, your church or a college basketball program. If you aren't moving forward, no matter the situation or circumstance, you are going to spiral backward—and quickly. In *Forward*, Pastor Jeremiah gives us a Bible-centered game plan and blueprint to keep moving our lives onward, upward, and forward."

—TOM CREAN
HEAD MEN'S BASKETBALL COACH, UNIVERSITY OF GEORGIA

"The world is paralyzed and panicked, but God's people were made for times like these. We don't just look forward, we push forward in the energy of Christ and with the foresight of biblical truth. Don't miss what's next for your life! The ink on these pages spills from the coffers of Dr. Jeremiah's biblical insights and life experiences. As you highlight his sentences, you'll sense how your future is highlighted with the golden glow of God's will. Thank you, Dr. J!"

—ROBERT J. MORGAN
AUTHOR AND SPEAKER

"As a coach and teacher of young people, I am thrilled that Dr. Jeremiah's new book, *Forward*, is so relatable to the struggles of today's athlete. Athletes have dreams and goals yet they deal with fear, doubt and distractions. This book turns that narrative upside down. Fear turns to courage and faith, doubt turns to purpose, and distractions turn to trusting God's plan for your life. I am anxious to share this book with athletes and witness the work that God is doing."

—PATTY GASSO
HEAD SOFTBALL COACH, THE UNIVERSITY OF OKLAHOMA

"Once again, Dr. Jeremiah has given us the message we need at the moment we need it the most. Powerful. Biblical. Inspirational. Practical."

—REV. JOHNNIE MOORE
PRESIDENT, THE CONGRESS OF CHRISTIAN LEADERS
AUTHOR OF *THE NEXT JIHAD*

"If you feel stuck now, you don't have to be. If you feel discouraged, it's time to deal with that. If you feel uncertain, you can get clarity. Dr. Jeremiah explains the process of how to find and fulfill God's dream for your life, and promises that because God exists, there is a reason for you to look forward to tomorrow."

—DR. JOHN ANKERBERG
AUTHOR AND SPEAKER
HOST OF *THE JOHN ANKERBERG SHOW*

"Brilliant. Biblical. Beautifully inspiring! *Forward*, by Dr David Jeremiah is a life-transforming journey to hope, help and the healthy direction to move your life toward the purpose, plan and unique path God has for your good and His glory. This book breathes *life* into your future!"

—PAM FARREL
AUTHOR OF BESTSELLING *MEN ARE LIKE WAFFLES,*
WOMEN ARE LIKE SPAGHETTI

"Can it be possible that God has a plan for your future? David Jeremiah tells us the answer is yes and that God wants you to fully embrace it. In his book *Forward*, he leads you to expectantly look for God's direction in your life and purpose for your future. It is such an encouraging read!"

—STEVE GREEN
PRESIDENT, HOBBY LOBBY

"How timely—so very timely! We must go forward—aware of His presence, secure in our relationship, unwavering in our commitment—pressing on no matter the cost. *Forward* will inspire and ready you for the challenge. At eighty-seven, I am pressing on because my Lord tells me there is no retirement, no discharge in the time of war (Ecc. 8:8). It's that time . . ."

—KAY ARTHUR
AUTHOR AND TEACHER
CO-FOUNDER AND AMBASSADOR OF PRECEPT MINISTRIES INTERNATIONAL

"From a new start to a strong finish, Dr. Jeremiah gives biblical and practical counsel on how to advance God's way. If you feel like you are stuck in a rut or just want to move to higher ground, *Forward* is the book to read now. Get ready to be inspired, challenged, and blessed!"

—SATISH KUMAR
FOUNDER AND PASTOR, CALVARY TEMPLE
HYDERABAD, INDIA

"I can't wait to pass *Forward* on to my teenagers, spouse, and parents because it has something crucial to say to every generation. We are all searching for answers and meaning in life, especially during troubling days in our world. As you read and apply this book, you'll not only find your purpose, you'll experience your heart coming to life again."

—ARLENE PELLICANE
SPEAKER AND PODCASTER
AUTHOR OF *PARENTS RISING*

"*Forward* outlines the kind of life that I want to live every day. Dr. Jeremiah has identified the biblical and practical steps, shared by both Christians and Jews, that help us see past the dizzying array of worries and distractions to the simple, straightforward path of a life devoted to God."

—YAEL ECKSTEIN
PRESIDENT AND CEO, THE INTERNATIONAL
FELLOWSHIP OF CHRISTIANS AND JEWS

Forward

*Discovering God's Presence and
Purpose in Your Tomorrow*

DR. DAVID JEREMIAH

W Publishing Group

An Imprint of Thomas Nelson

Published in Nashville, Tennessee, by W Publishing, an imprint of Thomas Nelson.

Published in association with Yates & Yates, www.yates2.com.

Thomas Nelson titles may be purchased in bulk for educational, business, fund-raising, or sales promotional use. For information, please email SpecialMarkets@ThomasNelson.com.

ISBN 978-0-7852-2411-2 (eBook)
ISBN 978-0-7852-3959-8 (IE)

Library of Congress Control Number: 2020942326

ISBN 978-0-7852-2402-0

Printed in the United States of America

20 21 22 23 24   LSC   10 9 8 7 6 5 4 3 2 1

To Tommy Walker
You wrote the song
that inspired this book.

Contents

Introduction

This book is about the rest of your life. It's about tomorrow. *Your* tomorrow—and the day after that.

Your God-given future is not a haphazard jumble of confusing contingencies. If you feel stuck, you don't have to be. If you feel discouraged, it's time to deal with that. If you feel uncertain, you can get clarity.

You're traveling an appointed way filled with promise and productivity. Everything in your past has prepared you for what's next, and every promise of God will provide what's needed. This is no time to let anxiety, apathy, or anything else hamper you.

I've written this book to encourage you to push forward, whatever your age or circumstances. Get on with your life and chase your unfolding future—and do it with focus, faith, and fervor. I'm excited about whatever is next for you! Your coming days and years are brimming with blessings. Yes, there may be burdens, but God knows about those too. So don't dread tomorrow. Leverage it for the Lord and for others.

I've lived long enough to learn something: no matter what season of life you're in, your best and brightest days are just around the corner. That's not just my opinion and it's not a pious platitude; it's biblical truth. When you seek first the kingdom of God and His righteousness, your future is always unfolding at the speed of grace. God is waiting to use you now more than ever, and your life is far from finished. It's just beginning.

Think of it this way. Your car's rearview mirror is a fraction of the size of the windshield, and there's a reason for that. Safe drivers glance in the mirror but focus on the road ahead. But how would you like to be the kind of driver preoccupied with the mirror? Too many people travel through life that way. They regret yesterday's failures, rehash yesterday's blessings, coast through life on a quarter-tank of fuel, and hope for a scenic overlook ahead. Too often that leaves them stalled by the side of the road.

Let me hand you a bucket and rag. Wash the windshield, buckle your seat belt, and shift the car into drive. That was the apostle Paul's attitude when he declared, "I focus on this one thing: Forgetting the past and looking *forward* to what lies ahead, I press on to reach the end of the race and receive the heavenly prize for which God, through Christ Jesus, is calling us" (Phil. 3:13–14 NLT).

That's been my approach to life too, but I felt a sense of rediscovery in this regard on Sunday, April 14, 2019. That evening at Shadow Mountain Community Church, where I serve, we invited musician Tommy Walker to minister to us in a concert. (To watch the song, go to https://vimeo.com/388291193/5c5f551a48.) Tommy is a gifted and heartfelt artist, and his last song grabbed my heart. It was as though he had written and sung that song just for me. Its title was "Forward," and the lyrics are, in part:

> It's been a long, long road
> It's been a crooked path
> With many twists and turns

But I'm not looking back
I'm walking straight ahead
Believing what You've said, Lord
That You're gonna be with me
No matter what life brings

Forward, I'm going forward
To the plans You have for me
To horizons yet unseen
Forward to Your new mercies I will find
As I'm pressing toward the prize
I'm going forward.[1]

In speaking with Tommy after the concert and later reading what he wrote about this song, I came to appreciate those words even more.

Tommy wrote, "This song was written with a sense of determination to move FORWARD by faith into the next season of my life. The older I get, the easier it is to want my life to be safe, comfortable, and predictable. But that's not God's plan! The God we worship is a God who loves the new and He's all about bringing newness to our lives and the lives of those around us."

Tommy continued, "We will have to let go of the safe and familiar in order to step into the things that bring His life, joy, and power! God desires that all of us press in and press on by faith to the good plans and good works he has for each of us! It's never too late! Let's say no to fear, complacency, and comfort and move FORWARD by faith in Jesus Name!"[2]

His song became the theme of this book.

Effective men and women are *forward* thinkers. The nineteenth-century preacher F. B. Meyer wrote, "It is a mistake to be always turning back to recover the past. The law for Christian living is not backward, but forward; not for experiences that lie behind, but for doing the will of God, which is always ahead and beckoning us to follow."

Meyer went on to urge us: "Leave the things that are behind, and reach forward to those that are before, for on each new height to which we attain, there are the appropriate joys that befit the new experience. Don't fret because life's joys are fled. There are more in front. Look up, press forward, the best is yet to be!"[3]

I've thought about this over and over, framing in my mind what that looks like for me. I believe there are ten actions that enable us to aggressively press forward in life: dream, pray, choose, focus, risk, pursue, believe, invest, finish, and celebrate. In this book, I've set forth each of them with a deep prayer that you'll share the excitement of living assertively in a forward direction.

This book is for young people who desperately need to know these things as they start moving into the fullness of God's will for them. It's for young parents and professionals stunned by the pressures of life. It's for those in midlife who need a fresh start. And it's for those of us who are older, because sometimes we forget that our richest moments of divine service are at hand.

Have you ever needed to jump-start your engine? The ten steps I describe in the pages that follow will spark your interest and help you move forward with fresh energy. It begins when you start to sense God's desires and dreams for you, which are birthed in prayer. As those dreams evolve in your heart, you declutter your routine so you can live with sharper focus and deeper faith. You latch on to the truth of God—that He has a unique road map for you and has wonderfully fashioned you for the route He's chosen.

In the process, you have to cast off pessimism and press onward with a positive mindset like that of the heroes in the book of Revelation who were ready to "follow the Lamb wherever he goes" (Rev. 14:4 NIV). Your life is an investment with eternal dividends. Here on earth, you'll finish in God's timing only to immediately resume your activities in heaven, where an eternity of worship, work, and fellowship awaits you.

In Jesus Christ your life is not obsolete, it's not out of fashion, and it's not over!

May the Lord Jesus use this book to help you discover—or to rediscover—the dreams, desires, and driving force He has waiting for you as you shift into following Him *forward*!

Chapter 1

Dream

Seize Your Tomorrow Today

When we think of great dreamers, we think of people like George Lucas, Elon Musk, or Walt Disney. Anyone who's seen a Star Wars movie, read about electric cars, or visited Disney World knows that great accomplishments begin with one person's larger-than-life imagination.

Walt Disney's dream began with cartoon sketches, two failed companies, and a borrowed book on animation. In time, he brought beloved characters to life, created classic films, and built Disney World, Disneyland, and Epcot. He created "the happiest place on earth" and became known as the man who made dreams come true.

Disney's public persona was "Uncle Walt," a smiling man who kindly signed autographs in a tweed jacket while puttering down Main Street in a fringe-topped car driven by Mickey Mouse. But behind the scenes, the real Walt Disney was a demanding, hard-charging man of a million ideas who exasperated family and colleagues. His life was a whirlwind of visionary projects that exhausted his associates and changed our world.

When Disney was diagnosed with lung cancer, he was still planning movies, developing theme parks, and mulling over his newest idea—an "Experimental Prototype Community of Tomorrow," or EPCOT. As he lay on his deathbed with his brother Roy sitting nearby, Walt looked up at the hospital ceiling tiles, raised his finger, and traced his plans for Epcot by pointing to them. Every fourth tile represented a square mile, he told his brother. Using that mental map, he suggested routes for his envisioned highways and monorails.[1]

Having said all that, I believe Walt Disney's dreams were too small. Believe it or not, you and I can dream bigger dreams than Disney ever conceived. It's one thing to invest one's life in a magic kingdom but quite another to play a part in the kingdom of God. As followers of Christ, we can cultivate a dream for our lives that outlasts the world, transforms time, changes eternity, and advances His cause and His kingdom for His glory.

In fact, that's the story of the Bible. The Bible is filled with people who saw what life could look like in God's kingdom and then moved forward in faith. Abraham dreamed of a great nation when he was yet childless. Moses envisioned a free people when the Israelites were still making bricks without straw. Joshua envisioned an occupied land; Samson, a defeated enemy; David, a temple on a hill. Nehemiah built miles of reconstructed walls in his prayers before a single stone was laid. Daniel glimpsed a future kingdom; Peter, an established church; Paul, a global mission.

All these stories—the dreams of men and women of God thousands of years ago—still inspire, guide, and affect us more than we know. And they remind us God wants to do the same with you and me. The Lord's dreams for us are just as real, and the process of finding and fulfilling them hasn't changed.

That's what this book is about. How do you stay focused on tomorrow, letting go of the past and moving forward to the future? What's the role of prayer? How do you figure out the next step? What's the risk? And what's waiting for you at the end of it all? In these pages I want to share with you these things—and more. I've never been content to hang up my boots and neither should you. There's always more out in front of us. Always a reason to look forward to tomorrow.

Typically, it all starts with a dream. That's the first step in this process of moving forward.

When I talk about a dream, I'm not describing a self-made vision of your life apart from God's will. And I'm not using the word as the ancient prophets did when they had supernatural visions of inspired revelation. I'm not talking about seeing heavenly creatures or having apocalyptic dreams. Instead, I'm talking about envisioning the next step or stage of your life. A dream or a vision is simply a picture of what you feel God wants you to do next.

What about you? What's your dream? Can you envision God's next step for your life? What does He want to do through you this year, in the coming years, and in the remaining time He gives you in this life?

The Power of a Dream

The Bible says, "Where there is no vision, the people perish" (Prov. 29:18 KJV). Without a blueprint, you can't build a house; and without an idea of what kind of house you want, a blueprint can't be drawn. The same is true when it comes to making plans for the future. If you don't have a clear idea about where you want to go—and why you want to go there—it's difficult to sustain forward momentum.

Without a dream, we float through life without ever catching the current. Many of us fill the majority of our hours with diversions and only a few with dreams. But our world is shaped by determined dreamers, by men and women of vision. Like them, you need a dream to achieve your goal.

Brett Hagler is someone who knows the power of a dream. After battling cancer in high school, Brett entered his twenties determined to make the most of life with lots of "gold, girls, and glory."

"I bought into the false equation that material things were going to bring me fulfillment. . . . It was the path to emptiness."

With the help of a friend, Hagler turned to Christ. Shortly afterward, he visited Haiti and saw the devastation from the 2010 earthquake. Hagler was reading the New Testament at the time, and he noticed how Jesus had a strong "bent and heart for the poor."

God gave Hagler a dream to establish a nonprofit company called New Story, a housing start-up that uses 3D printing machines to create homes. New Story can build a two-bedroom, one bath home in about 24 hours! Goldman Sachs calls Hagler one of the Top 100 Most Intriguing Entrepreneurs as he seeks to combat global homelessness.

Today when Brett travels the country telling people about his story, he encourages audiences with a simple but powerful motto: dream big, but start small.[2] That's great advice!

I admire people who envision things not yet seen and do things not yet done. Imagineers open the door to the future and let us in. Their names fill the chapters of our history books: Alexander the Great, Nicolaus Copernicus, Leonardo Da Vinci, Christopher Columbus, Thomas Edison, Albert Einstein, Neil Armstrong, Steve Jobs, Mary Anderson.

Mary Anderson? Who's she?

She was an ordinary woman who visited New York City during the winter of 1902. The snow and ice were coming down furiously, and when Mary hopped on a streetcar she noticed the driver had to keep the front window open because the windshield was covered with snow. Returning home, she envisioned a rubber device that would sweep back and forth over the windshield to keep it clear for driving. She invented the windshield wiper.[3]

You see, everyone can have vision—young or old, rich or poor, famous or obscure. Whether you dream of peering through portholes or windshields, you need to be gazing into the future and asking God what He wants you to do next.

Build Your Dream

Jan Koum was born into a Jewish family in Kiev, Ukraine, in 1976, during the Soviet era when anti-Semitism was rampant. There was no running water in their home, and his parents were seldom together because of work. They assumed their phone was tapped, so they had limited contact with the world. Jan grew up with a constant feeling of being bugged and surveilled.

When he was sixteen, Jan and his mother immigrated to California. (His dad planned to come later but died before he could make the trip.) Jan's mother found work as a babysitter, and Jan swept floors to help pay bills. When he got his first computer in high school, he taught himself programming by buying used computer manuals. That skill led to a job as an internet security tester, and later he was hired by Yahoo.

One evening Jan visited the home of Alex Fishman, who often invited the local Russian community to his home for pizza and movies. Forty or so people showed up, and that's where Jan's dream was born. He wanted a way for people to stay in touch without Big Brother listening—an encrypted phone app. Apps were a new thing, and Jan had bought his first iPhone and visited one of the first app stores a few months before. He wondered if an app could actually help people stay in touch around the world. He remembered the difficulty of communicating with his family in Ukraine and the expense involved. He also shuddered as he thought of being monitored. Koum began to envision an app that would safely connect people around the world.

He thought of the name WhatsApp because it sounded like "What's up." Jan found some cheap cubicles in a converted warehouse and worked day and night, covering himself in blankets to stay warm. Instead of making money, he drained his bank account. This was during the great recession of 2009. Who launches a start-up in a downturn?

Still, Jan Koum and his partner from Yahoo days, Brian Acton, worked on. "We won't stop until every single person on the planet has an affordable and reliable way to communicate with their friends and loved ones," Jan promised.[4]

When Jan Koum sold WhatsApp to Facebook for $19.3 billion in 2014, he chose an unusual place to sign the papers: an old white building that used to house the social services office in the California town where Jan went to school. He and his mother had stood in line in front of that same building to collect food stamps.[5]

When Jan Koum had nothing, he actually had the one thing many people never find: he had a dream. Despite hardship, and against great odds, the vision of a better tomorrow drove him forward in life. That's what a dream can do for you, and you don't need a computer, a movie studio, or a theme park to realize it. All you need is a picture of what your tomorrow could be as you follow Christ.

Lillian Trasher had that kind of dream. At the beginning of the last century, Lillian was working in an orphanage in North Carolina when she felt God's call to pursue missionary work in Egypt. The call was so strong that she broke off her engagement when her fiancé did not share her vision. She sold her belongings and boldly booked passage to a foreign country, arriving with less than a hundred dollars in her purse. One day she was asked to go to the bedside of a dying young widow, who begged Lillian to care for her malnourished baby girl. Lillian agreed, and so began the first orphanage in Egypt.

Those first years were filled with great difficulty and limited support, but Lillian persevered to realize her vision of not only an orphanage but also schools and evangelistic ministries. By the time of her death in 1961, Lillian had cared for more than eight thousand orphans and touched thousands of others. The organization she founded, the Lillian Trasher Orphanage, still serves the needy in Egypt today.

For me, the best part of Lillian's story was the prayer she offered to the Lord when yet a child. She never forgot it, nor did the Lord. She said: "Lord, I want to be your little girl. Lord, if ever I can do anything for You, just let me know and I'll do it!"[6]

Can you think of a simpler prayer than that? Try it! *Lord, if ever I can do anything for You, just let me know and I'll do it.*

So if vision is so important, how do you build your own? There are many biblical models you could follow, but I believe the best example of dream-building in the Bible is the story of King David's vision to build a temple for the Lord atop Jerusalem's Mount Moriah.

For hundreds of years, Israel had worshiped around the frayed remains of the tabernacle, the elaborate tent constructed in the days of Moses as a portable house of worship. But now the nation was occupying the land God had promised, and Jerusalem was its capital. So David began dreaming of a permanent place where people could worship for centuries to come.

David's story reveals the principles you and I can follow as we build our own dreams.

Root Your Dream in History

In 2 Samuel 7, David told the prophet Nathan, "See now, I dwell in a house of cedar, but the ark of God dwells inside tent curtains" (v. 2). Nathan's initial reaction was positive—go ahead and do it. So David grabbed hold of his dream and began moving forward to see its fulfillment.

But David's idea to build a temple didn't just "poof" into his head like an exploding nebula. It was rooted in the history of Israel. Centuries before, God told Abraham to offer his son, Isaac, as a sacrifice and burnt offering on a distant mountain. And God was specific about the mountain. Not just any hilltop would do. It had to be Mount Moriah (Gen. 22:2).

A thousand years later, when David and then Solomon planned to build the Jewish temple, they placed it on that very mountain, Mount Moriah (2 Chron. 3:1). David's vision for the location of his temple had roots as deep as Genesis 22. It was grounded in the story of Abraham's willingness to sacrifice his only begotten son as a burnt offering (Heb. 11:17–19). It's no coincidence that a thousand years after David, Jesus Christ gave Himself as an offering for sin on or near this very ridge.

From Abraham and his son, to David and his temple, to Christ and His cross—everything was linked, and each event had its roots in the one that preceded it.

The best dreams don't start with us but instead are planted in us by God. If it isn't rooted, it's rotten. We stand on the shoulders of others. We are links in a chain, and we build on what others have done, even as future generations will build on the work we have done.

That's why it's all right to look around for ideas and see what others are doing. We get ideas from history and from how others are inspired to act today. To develop your dream, think about your heritage, what you love to do, and your life experiences. Think about your background. Everything in your life has prepared you for the next step, so look at what's already happening in your life and church. Start where you are and work outward and forward.

Brewster McLeod was a pastor at Southland Christian Church in Lexington, Kentucky, for forty years. In 2000, he saw that many special-needs students were inadvertently excluded from their high school prom. So he organized a prom event just for them in a local church. That experience fueled McLeod's burden for special-needs kids, and the focus of his ministry shifted to serving those with special needs. For the past two decades he's ministered to this group in the name of Christ.

Last year, the now-retired pastor brought his vision to life in a new way—he opened a nonprofit coffee shop that employs fifty young people with autism and developmental difficulties. The coffee shop provides income and purpose for the employees, whom he calls VIPs, and it helps integrate them into the community by allowing customers the chance to grow comfortable with those with special needs.

"I don't do it for that pat on the back because that can be very addicting," McLeod says. "I do it because I really care about them and I know that they are gifted. I just want them to know they have great value."[7]

Brewster McLeod saw a need that moved his heart, and he responded by doing something that came naturally to him, something he'd been doing for years—he organized an event in a church. And from there his dream kept growing.

Future vision comes from past ventures. The new is built on the old. As you ponder and pray about your personal dreams, think back over your life, your experiences, your mentors and influencers, your gifts, and your passions. Root your dream in history, and you will have a firm foothold on which to move forward.

Reproduce Your Dream in a Picture

As ideas and intentions bubble up in your heart and mind, you need to figure out where to begin and how to implement your dream. You have to nudge the abstract burden into a real-life plan. After all, for your vision to touch others it must become as practical as Esther's dinner, David's slingshot, Gideon's torches, the boy's lunch of bread and fish, the Good Samaritan's wine and oil, Philemon's hospitality, Dorcas's robes, and Paul's pen and parchment. We never know how a single detail, born from a visionary mind, will be used by the Lord in helping this world.

Visionaries have an uncanny ability to "see" their dreams and convey them in images. That's how David built the impetus needed for his temple project. As we have seen, David's dream began when he told the prophet Nathan, "See now, I dwell in a house of cedar, but the ark of God dwells inside tent curtains" (2 Sam. 7:2). The temple wasn't an abstract concept but a vision that filled his mind in technicolor. He was able to convey that image to others and motivate them to action by drawing a contrast: "Look at my palace with its paneled walls and glorious bulwarks, and look at that frayed tent called the tabernacle. Shouldn't God's house be better than any home of yours or mine?"

The ability to see what could be is essential to straining forward toward the realization of your dream. At the funeral of Steve Jobs, his wife, Laurene Powell, said: "It is hard enough to see what is already there, to remove the many impediments to a clear view of reality, but Steve's gift was even greater: he saw clearly what was not there, what could be there, what had to be there. His mind was never a captive of reality. Quite the contrary. He imagined what reality lacked, and he set out to remedy it."[8]

That's so important. As a pastor, I've been involved in ten building programs during my career. By God's grace, I've been able to picture each of the buildings in my mind before they showed up in blueprints, scale models, or erected structures. I don't know how you can fulfill a vision unless you see it in your prayers and dreams.

One day Edwin Land was sightseeing in New Mexico with his three-year-old granddaughter, and they were taking pictures of things that interested them. The little girl was impatient to see how the pictures turned out. She wanted to know why she couldn't see them instantly. Land took a short walk in the desert and pondered that question. By the time he returned, he had visualized a camera that would develop its negatives instantly. He saw the whole thing in his mind, and he went on to invent the Polaroid Land Camera, one of the most successful photographic products of the twentieth century. Describing how he invented the camera, Land later said, "You always start with a fantasy. Part of the fantasy technique is to visualize something as perfect. Then with the experiments you work back from the fantasy to reality, hacking away at the components."[9]

Having a dream for tomorrow isn't just a matter of feeling a generalized burden. It may start there, with a yearning to feed the hungry, help the homeless, or evangelize the world. But as your vision develops, it takes on distinct and detailed images. You can see yourself rolling up your sleeves and getting a grip on the very things needed to press forward with your dream. You can convey it to others in a way that excites them.

Don't worry if you can't see the final fulfillment of your long-term dreams—we will walk through the practical steps toward reaching success in the chapters to come. For now, what matters is being able to imagine your dream in a way that captivates both you and others.

Reinforce Your Dream with Determination

David also discovered that every dream faces discouragement. That's part of the process of proving its validity. David's dream for the temple excited him like nothing else in his life. He was fired up, ready to go, eager to lead the campaign to build. He could see it in his mind's eye every time he looked from his palace rooftop toward Mount Moriah.

But then the roof caved in, so to speak. God told David he would not be allowed to build the temple because of his violent past: "You shall not build a house for My name, because you have been a man of war and have shed blood. . . . It is your son Solomon who shall build My house and My courts" (1 Chron. 28:3, 6). Talk about the death of a vision!

Oh, how many of my visions have died, and each time it feels like a small part of my heart dies. I have a little place near my home where I go and park my car and pout a little when a dream of mine doesn't pan out. I think through it, surrender things to God's will, and then drive away looking forward through the windshield, not backward in the rearview mirror.

But David didn't pout for long, if at all. He told himself something like this: "Well, if I can't do it myself, and if God has appointed the task for my son Solomon, then I'll do all I can to help him succeed." In refusing to give up on the project because he was taken out of the driver's seat, David illustrated a core value of dream building: no dream is ever realized without a huge measure of determination.

It reminds me of a story about my oldest grandson, David Todd. One of our family Christmas traditions is assembling jigsaw puzzles. This year David Todd joined in. He enjoyed it so much that he told his roommates about it when he got back to college, and they decided to tackle a puzzle together. To my amazement, they bought a two-thousand-piece puzzle.

It took ten days for them to finish the puzzle around their regular obligations. Then I got a phone call from a very frustrated David Todd. He told me the puzzle was done, but the very last piece was missing!

So what did he and his friends do? Determined to complete what they started, they went back to the store and bought the very same puzzle. Using the box top as a guide, they searched through all two thousand pieces until they found the culprit. With great satisfaction, they snapped that final piece into place. The completed puzzle now hangs on their wall, bearing the signatures of everyone who helped.

The puzzle was a fun project, a simple, shared goal among friends. But their determination to achieve that goal was real. The picture on the box top was both vision and guide, showing them their goal as well as the exact puzzle piece they needed to achieve it. God's vision is a guide for you to follow too. And when God places His dream in your heart, you become more determined and dedicated. You press on to see the work finished.

In the Bible, a young widow named Ruth who lived in Moab was devoted to her mother-in-law, Naomi. When Naomi decided to return to Bethlehem after her husband and sons died, Ruth wanted to accompany her. Naomi tried to dissuade her, but the Bible says that when Naomi "saw that she was determined to go with her," she yielded and took her along (Ruth 1:18). They arrived in Bethlehem, where Ruth gleaned fallen barley and wheat from the fields of Naomi's relative Boaz to make their bread. Eventually she married Boaz, and their son became the grandfather of King David, and thus part of the family line of Jesus Christ.

Having a deep conviction of what we feel God wants us to do for eternity will make us men and women of devotion, dedication, and determination. When we are determined to do our part for God, the pieces of the puzzle magnificently come together.

Reconcile Your Dream with Its Cost

As you build your vision, be willing to sacrifice. Dreams are costly, as David found out when God led him to purchase some land for the temple at a high spot in the area. It was owned by Araunah the Jebusite, who used the high location for its winds to thresh out his wheat. The chaff would blow away, and the grains of wheat would be collected and sold. David approached Araunah for this valuable site, the most desirable location in Jerusalem.

Because he was the venerable king of Israel, David could have seized the land, and that may be why Araunah offered to donate it to him. But David said, "No, but I will surely buy it from you for a price; nor will I offer burnt offerings to the LORD my God with that which costs me nothing" (2 Sam. 24:24).

Big dreams are expensive. If you've experienced a fulfilled dream, you know what I'm talking about. The cost comes in money, energy, criticism, unbelief, unplanned obstructions, unfaithful helpers, and a multitude of other discouraging things.

I think Jesus was trying to help us with all of this when He wrote these words: "For which of you, intending to build a tower, does not sit down first and count the cost, whether he has enough to finish it. . . . Or what king, going to make war against another king, does not sit down first and consider whether he is able with ten thousand to meet him who comes against him with twenty thousand?" (Luke 14:28, 31).

Your dream might not involve building a tower or going to war, but there is still a cost involved if you want to see it through. Not understanding that cost up front can cause you to give up on your dream when you hit the first hurdle.

Dorothea Dix was a woman who understood the cost of a dream. Dorothea, who was born in Maine in 1802, ran away from home at age twelve to escape her alcoholic family and abusive father. She lived with her grandmother in Boston, and by age fourteen she was teaching in a school for girls. Eventually she was asked to teach a Sunday school class of women in a prison housing the insane and mentally disturbed, who, at that time, were jailed alongside criminals and treated like animals. Many of these souls were cold and naked, kept in darkness, chained to the walls, and even flogged.

Dorothea determined with all her heart to help these wretched castaways from society, and she devoted the rest of her life to a relentless vision for prison reform for the mentally ill. She visited penitentiaries, filed reports, testified before legislatures, wrote articles, gave speeches, and initiated reforms. She visited hundreds of prisons and jails, and everywhere she went, she grappled with a level of suffering that sickened her.

In her trademark bonnet and cashmere shawl, Dorothea logged more than sixty thousand miles by train and carriage, testifying that God's providence was defining her path. Horace Mann said she had a "divine magnetism."

Dorothea was among the first American reformers to speak up for mentally ill children. And when her proposals were voted down in state legislatures, she redoubled her efforts. Traveling abroad, she championed prison reform for the mentally disabled across Britain and throughout Europe. When the Civil War broke out in America, she was named Chief of Army Nurses for the Union and wore herself out organizing medical care for wounded soldiers. When the war ended, she was sixty-three years old and weighed ninety-five pounds, but she was far from finished.

Dorothea hit the road again on behalf of the mentally ill, spending another fifteen years traveling between Maine and California, establishing ministries for society's forgotten victims. "It would seem all my work is never to be done," she wrote. Yet she kept working.

For the last fifty years of her life, Dorothea had no home. She simply lived in the quarters of the 123 asylums and hospitals she had founded. She passed away at age eighty-five, and Matthew 25:35–36 was read at her funeral: "I was hungry and you gave Me food; I was thirsty and you gave Me drink; I was a stranger and you took Me in; I was naked and you clothed Me; I was sick and you visited Me; I was in prison and you came to Me."[10]

Dorothea paid a huge price in pursuing her dream, but she also received a great reward—namely, improvements across the globe in the treatment of millions of people suffering from mental illness. The cost she paid for her efforts was real, but the benefits are still rippling through our world today.

Release Your Dream to Your Legacy

Looking back on this period of Israel's history, one thing jumps out at me: this was David's dream, but it ended up being called Solomon's temple. Amazingly, David not only accepted that—he made it happen.

David refused to allow his dream to die when he died. And although he was not allowed to build the temple, the Lord nevertheless gave him the construction details, which he passed on to his son Solomon. In 1 Chronicles 28:10–12 we read:

> "Consider now, for the LORD has chosen you to build a house for the
> sanctuary; be strong, and do it." Then David gave his son Solomon the
> plans for the vestibule, its houses, its treasuries, its upper chambers,

its inner chambers, and the place of the mercy seat; and the plans for all that he had by the Spirit, of the courts of the house of the LORD, of all the chambers all around, of the treasuries of the house of God, and of the treasuries for the dedicated things.

The Holy Spirit had instructed David with the specific details of the temple, and David in turn passed them on to his son. I can imagine David transferring the information from God onto an architectural blueprint, then laying it out before Solomon and saying, "Here it is. God gave this to me. This is what you are to build."

David had dreamed of building a permanent place where God could be worshiped, and he determined to leave something behind that would honor the Lord. It was his dream and the resources he put in place that allowed his son Solomon to move quickly toward the construction of the temple.

David's instructions to Solomon have been a charge to pastors, missionaries, and Christian workers ever since: "Be strong and of good courage, and do it; do not fear nor be dismayed, for the LORD God—my God—will be with you. He will not leave you nor forsake you, until you have finished all the work for the service of the house of the LORD" (1 Chron. 28:20).

This story also illustrates how it's possible to achieve something after your death that could not have been achieved during your life. Before he died, David decided to pass on something that would live on after him. From his life we can learn the great importance of dreaming beyond the span of our years. How can God use us? What is something He could do through each of us after we are gone?

I often think about this when I hold the *Jeremiah Study Bible* in my hands. I remember as a young boy reading the *Scofield Reference Bible* that my parents gave me for my sixteenth birthday. It was part of my spiritual education. I still have that Bible and I cherish it. It was the standard reference Bible during my growing-up years even though it was copyrighted in 1909. Years after its inception, it was still helping people like me understand what the Bible says, what the Bible means, and what the Bible means for me.

I can only hope and pray that in some small way the *Jeremiah Study Bible*, which was released in 2013, will have that same impact on some future student of the Scriptures.

One Sunday afternoon in 1771, a man named Valentin Haüy ducked into a restaurant in Paris for dinner. He sat near the stage, and the show that evening featured blind people in a comedy routine. They were objects of ridicule and cruelty. The act was designed to make fun of their blindness. Deeply offended, Haüy began to develop a burden for the blind.

Sometime later, he spotted a sightless street urchin who was begging for coins outside a Parisian church. Giving the boy some money, Haüy was amazed to see the boy feel the raised markings on the coins and distinguish the amounts. That gave Haüy an idea. Why couldn't books be written with raised letters, like images on coins? Why couldn't people learn to read with their fingers? Haüy took the boy off the streets, offered him food and shelter, devised a plan with wooden blocks and numbers, and taught the boy to read. In 1784, Haüy started the world's first school for blind children. It was in Paris, and one of the first teachers was the blind boy rescued from the streets.

But that's just the beginning.

Several years later, another boy named Louis was born in the village of Coupvray, France. His father was a farmer and harness maker, and as a toddler Louis loved watching his father work with leather tools. But tragedy struck in 1812 when three-year-old Louis was playing with a leftover strap of leather, trying to punch holes in it. His hand slipped, and the sharp tool punctured and put out his eye. An infection set in that spread to the other eye, and little Louis ended up blinded in both eyes for life.

A local minister named Jacques Palluy loved the boy and began visiting him to read him the Bible. Seeing the boy had a good mind,

Father Jacques determined he should receive an education. So at age ten, Louis was enrolled in the school Haüy had established in Paris, where he proved to be a brilliant student.

Eventually Louis began teaching other students in the Paris School for the Blind. He studied Haüy's method of reading, and he also became aware of a system of military communication developed by a French army captain that allowed soldiers to communicate in the dark by running their fingers over a series of dots and dashes. Though still a teenager, Louis Braille began adapting these systems into a program of his own; in 1829, at age twenty, he published a little book on the Braille method of reading.

The school resided in a damp building by the River Seine. It was cold and unhealthy, and the food and conditions were poor. Louis developed tuberculosis, but he continued working on his system of reading, which began catching on and soon was being exported around the world. As his health failed, Louis said, "I am convinced my mission on earth has been accomplished. I asked God to carry me away from this world."[11]

Think of the chain reaction of that cascading dream. One man developed a burden for the blind when he saw ridiculed actors on stage and a beggar boy on the streets. His burden led him to establish a school and attempt a system of reading. Then a local pastor developed a burden for a blind boy in another village and taught him the Bible and longed to send him to school. That blind child, Louis Braille, developed a burden to improve and to expand Haüy's work. The world was changed, and as a result, millions of sightless souls have experienced the joy of reading the Bible and other books for themselves for almost two centuries.

You and I may never create a language for the blind or build a temple for the Lord, but please remember there are no small tasks in the Lord's work, and no insignificant dreams. Our work is never routine, our labor is never wasted, and our legacy is capable of outliving us.

You Can Trust God with Your Dreams

I've always loved radio and everything about radio. From sitting next to the radio as a child with my ear to the speaker so I could listen to *The Lone Ranger* or *The Shadow*, to putting together Knight radio kits as a teenager. For reasons I cannot explain, radio has had a mysterious hold over me as far back as I can remember.

When I became a student at Cedarville College in 1959, I was given the radio opportunity of a lifetime. A new Christian FM station was being launched in Springfield, Ohio, just fifteen miles from my home. I don't remember how it happened, but I was able to audition for an on-air announcing position, and I got the job.

Every day, Monday through Friday, I drove to Springfield to do the 3:00 p.m. to 11:00 p.m. shift on WEEC-FM. I did the news, hosted call-in music shows, and cued up and played radio programs like *Back to the Bible* and *Unshackled*. I loved every minute of it, and when I was asked to help start a radio station on our college campus, I teamed up with Paul Gathany, a college classmate, and my girlfriend—and soon-to-be wife—Donna Thompson, and we launched WCDR-FM. This station had a humble beginning. It was a twelve-watt transmitter on the third floor of the administration building. We used to joke with each other that on a good day you could hear the station on the first floor.

In time that station grew to a network of stations that literally covered the entire Ohio Miami Valley with great Christian music and the message of the gospel. I believe God used WCDR to help grow Cedarville College.

When I was a college junior, God called me into the ministry. It was absolutely, definitely clear to me that I was to become a preacher of the gospel, so I immediately enrolled in Dallas Theological Seminary. Donna and I got married right after graduation, and we headed off to Texas for four years of post-graduate training.

My greatest regret, if I could call it that, was this: I loved radio and had spent most of my life involved with radio. Yet now it appeared God was leading me in a totally different direction in terms of my vocation and lifelong calling.

Radio was put on hold for four years while I worked on my master's degree, but what happened after that is one of the most amazing stories of my life. After a short stint as a youth pastor in New Jersey and twelve years as a pastor of a start-up church in Fort Wayne, Indiana, I accepted the call to Shadow Mountain Community Church (at that time called Scott Memorial Baptist Church) in San Diego, California. The next year I began a local five-day-a-week teaching program on a Christian station in San Diego, Salem Radio's KPRZ. The station manager, David Ruleman, helped me get started in this new format . . . and the rest is history.

Today *Turning Point* hits the airwaves on more than three thousand radio stations in the United States, and on many of those stations the program is heard two or three times per day. *Momento Decisivo*, the Spanish edition of the program, is heard in every country where Spanish is spoken. We broadcast more than 121,000 radio programs and 4,050 television programs outside the United States each year—in languages including Bahasa, Hindi, and Mandarin.

So you can see that God did not call me into the ministry to take my dream away. He called me into the ministry because my dream was way too small! He had a much better and a much bigger plan for my life.

As a result of those experiences, I've learned I can trust God with my dreams even as I move forward toward His plans for my life.

And so can you.

Chapter 2

Pray

Consult with Your Creator

In 1909, young Leonora Wood volunteered to go to the Appalachian Mountains to teach in a one-room mission school. There, in the impoverished town of Del Rio, Tennessee, she became something of a living legend thanks to her deep faith in the power of prayer. Leonora knew how to turn dreams into prayer and prayer into dreams, and she believed we must step toward our goals in God's presence through prayer.

Raymond Thomas was a foster teen who often stopped at Leonora's cabin in his knee-high clodhoppers to talk with her as she sat on the front porch shelling peas or darning socks. Raymond's seemingly impossible dream was to go to college.

"But how can I manage it? I've no money saved. Nor any prospects," he said.

"Raymond," Leonora replied, "whatever you need, God has the supply ready for you, provided you're ready to receive it. . . . The money will be there for any dream that's right for you, every dream for which you're willing to work."

Raymond asked Leonora to offer a "dreaming prayer" for him, and her prayer went like this: "Father, You've given Raymond a fine mind. We believe You want that mind to be developed, that You want Raymond's potential to be used to help You lift and lighten some portion of Your world. Since all the wealth of the world is Yours, please help Raymond find everything he needs for an education."

But she wasn't done.

"And Father, we also believe you have even bigger plans for Raymond. Plant in his mind and heart the vivid pictures, the specific dreams that reflect Your plans for him after college. And oh, give him joy in dreaming—great joy."

Raymond Thomas did make it through college in four years, working *twelve* jobs to support himself and graduating with a Bachelor of Science degree *cum laude*. He also served in World War II and later settled in Vienna, where he earned a PhD in Physics. He went on to visit sixty countries, master multiple languages, and network with some of the most important people in Europe through his job with the US Atomic Energy Commission.

Years later, Leonora's daughter, Catherine Marshall, wrote Raymond that she was coming to Europe. When Catherine arrived in Rome, she found officials ready to show her sacred sites few tourists can access. In Florence, she was taken to the top of the dome of the Duomo. In Venice, a gondola awaited her. Catherine realized her childhood friend was known across Europe.

When they finally met in Vienna, Raymond told her, "The fact that I could sit on your front steps and—with no money at all—dream of going to college and achieve it, proved something to me. Very simply, what your mother said was true—any right dream can be realized. . . . And prayer helps you know if it is right and gives you the power to stay with it."[1]

That's what Nehemiah would say too.

Nehemiah was one of the most effective leaders in the Bible, and his story unfolds in the Old Testament book that bears his name. Executives and entrepreneurs endlessly study his book because of the leadership lessons it contains.

Nehemiah was a Jewish official serving the Persian king in the city of Susa, a thousand miles from Jerusalem, which at the time was a ruined city. The Babylonians had destroyed Israel and Jerusalem in 587 BC, but several thousand Hebrew settlers had finally returned to rebuild the temple and reestablish a Jewish presence there.

This was a deep burden for Nehemiah. He knew God's plan of redemption depended on the continuity of His people in their land, where they could offer sacrifices in His temple and await His Messiah. To Nehemiah, it was a matter of heartfelt prayer.

One day, Nehemiah's brother and a few other men arrived in Susa with grim news from Jerusalem. "Those who survived the exile and are back in the province are in great trouble and disgrace," they told Nehemiah. "The wall of Jerusalem is broken down, and its gates have been burned with fire" (Neh. 1:3 NIV).

The news hit Nehemiah like a blast. Slumping into his chair, he started sobbing. But out of his deep tears came earnest prayers, and out of his prayers came a fervent dream. With God's help, he himself would return to Jerusalem and rebuild the walls of the ancient city of His God. It seemed an impossible feat because Nehemiah was the king's cupbearer and a trusted advisor. The likelihood of King Artaxerxes releasing him (let alone financing the trip) seemed far-fetched. But God had already planted the dream in Nehemiah's heart, just as He is planting fresh dreams in yours.

Prepare Your Heart for God's Plan

God's desires flourish in prepared hearts, just like seeds in furrowed ground. In the last chapter I urged you to imagine your future. If you're saying, "Yes! I want to do that!" but you're not certain what your dream is, or what the next step forward is, then prayer is the answer.

Nehemiah saw a need that burdened his heart and started praying about it. I've studied the book of Nehemiah for years, and there are two verses that tell us something about dreams—not the kind you have at night but the kind that guide you forward.

Notice these two telling phrases: Nehemiah claimed that God "put in my heart" to rebuild the walls of Jerusalem (Neh. 2:12 NIV). Later he said, "my God put it into my heart" to organize the people (Neh. 7:5 NIV).

Remember Leonora Wood's prayer: *plant in his mind and heart the vivid pictures, the specific dreams that reflect Your plans.*

That's what happened to Nehemiah. He didn't come up with his dream for Jerusalem's walls all by himself. His heart was receptive to the burdens and impressions God sent him. A prayerful heart is fertile ground for divine ideas.

Chip Barker will tell you about that over a plate of Texas brisket. Several years ago he lost his job with Pepsi when the local distribution center closed. His wife, Karen, was laid off at the same time. "We got behind on everything," Chip said. "We were borrowing money from every Tom, Dick, and Harry we could find just to pay our electric bill."

Barker hired himself out for yard work, and his wife did the same for housework.

One morning, Barker grabbed a cup of coffee and walked among the pecan trees behind his house. He started praying, asking God to give him a dream and show him what to do. He said, "Lord, I don't want to do what I'm doing. I need You to show me the way."

A line from a well-known movie, *Field of Dreams*, came to his mind: "If you build it, they will come." Chip pondered that a moment, then dismissed it and continued praying. Nearby, the neighbors were cooking bacon for breakfast, and the smell drifted through the pecan trees. Then and there, Chip decided to open a barbecue restaurant.

That night he couldn't sleep, so he headed to a local convenience store for another cup of coffee. While there, he met a friend who suggested keeping it simple, running his restaurant out of a storage shed. Chip calculated the costs and determined he needed $12,000.

"God's behind it!" he told himself, driving to the local bank. He was approved for the loan, and he signed the papers beneath the pecan trees where he'd prayed for guidance. That was years ago, and today Chipster's Grill is known across Texas for its food and fellowship.[2]

How can you be sure the dream in your heart is God's will, not yours? You must humbly and specifically ask God to place His ideas for your life into your heart and mind. Psalm 25:4 says, "Show me Your ways, O LORD; teach me Your paths."

The sooner you do that, the better. Thank God for teenagers like Raymond Thomas who know how to pray a "dreaming prayer" while they're young, and for people like Chip Barker who do it later. No matter your age, don't worry. It's never too soon or too late to ask God for the next chapter in your life. It's never too soon or too late to move forward!

A perfect example is Fred Lunsford, who was one of the soldiers who stormed the beaches of Normandy on D-Day in 1944. After the war, he became a pastor in the mountains of North Carolina, where he devoted seventy faithful years to preaching the gospel.

Two years ago when Lunsford was ninety-three, he became very sick and thought he would die. He told the Lord he wanted to go to heaven, but God said, "Not yet!'"

Sitting in the prayer garden behind his house, Lunsford asked the Lord, "Why are you leaving me here?"

The Lord seemed to answer by saying He had some "unfinished business" for Lunsford to do—"To pray for a spiritual awakening!"

From that moment, Lunsford has been earnestly praying for an awakening in America and around the world, and he's recruiting others to do the same. Recently Fox News carried a story about him, reporting that somehow—don't ask me how—Lunsford has well over a quarter-million people praying with him every day for a great out-pouring of revival.

"This is truly a revival of prayer," Lunsford said. "From this day forward, God's going to do wonders. What it is, I don't know, but I want to be a part of it."[3]

Me too! God put His dreams into the heart of an impoverished foster teen in Appalachia, into the mind of an unemployed man under a grove of pecan trees in Texas, into the soul of a ninety-three-year-old veteran in his prayer garden, and into the heart of a cupbearer of ancient Susa. Never doubt that He can surely show you what He wants you to do next.

Pray right now with the psalmist: "Show me Your ways, O LORD; teach me Your paths" (Ps. 25:4).

Pray About Your Plans Day and Night

No matter the hour or the circumstances, pray! As God begins to give you impressions and thoughts about your future, commit them to Him in serious, ongoing prayer. As soon as Nehemiah sensed the need for rebuilding the walls of Jerusalem, he "mourned and fasted and prayed before the God of heaven" (Neh. 1:4 NIV).

As his thoughts clarified and he better understood what needed to happen, he wrote out an earnest prayer, preserved for us in Nehemiah 1:5–11. He began: "LORD, the God of heaven, the great and awesome God, who keeps his covenant of love with those who love him and keep his commandments, let your ear be attentive and your eyes open to hear the prayer your servant is praying before you day and night" (vv. 5–6 NIV).

Nehemiah went on to confess his sins and those of his people. He reminded God of the biblical promises involving the children of Israel. Then he ended by saying: "LORD, let your ear be attentive to the prayer of this your servant and to the prayer of your servants who delight in revering your name. Give your servant success today by granting him favor in the presence of this man" (v. 11 NIV).

Who was "this man"? He was King Artaxerxes, the most powerful man on earth. Even though Nehemiah was his cupbearer, he couldn't approach the king without risking his life. Only God could arrange the right moment. So Nehemiah prayed.

Many Christians have forgotten how to pray earnestly and with fervor. When did you last pour yourself into an earnest season of prayer? We get too busy, don't we?

E. M. Bounds was a nineteenth-century pastor who wrote inspiring books on the subject of prayer. Every page is so convicting I can only read him in small doses. Bounds called prayer "spiritual energy."

> How vast are the possibilities of prayer! How wide its reach! What great things are accomplished by this divinely appointed means of grace! It lays its hand on Almighty God and moves Him to do what He would not otherwise do if prayer were not offered. It brings things to pass which would never otherwise occur. The story of prayer is the story of great achievements. Prayer is a wonderful power placed by Almighty God in the hands of his saints, which may be used to accomplish great purposes and to achieve unusual results.[4]

Nehemiah certainly believed that. So does Mark Cole, a well-known worship leader with more than one hundred published songs in his portfolio. Cole has spent his career training musicians and discipling Christians.

In the fall of 1981, Mark was the music director for a Christian band in Europe. He was twenty-seven, single, traveling from one country to the next with the message of Christ. He looked forward to ministering behind the Iron Curtain, but the Solidarity strikes in Poland thwarted his plans. He ended up staying a month in a Christian hostel near Vienna.

While there, Cole started reading his Bible with renewed zeal. The Lord used those weeks in Austria to work deeply in his heart. He also happened to watch a video by a New Zealand teacher named Winkie Pratney. The subject was: "How to Find a Wife." The talk was based on Genesis 24, where Abraham sent his servant to find a wife for Isaac. Pratney pointed out how the servant had asked for God's guidance, and how the servant had bumped into just the right girl for the hapless Isaac.

"That sounded good to me," said Cole, "so I drew up a list of nineteen things that I was looking for in a wife. I was very specific. . . . Over the next few months God continued to work on my heart and transform me. I don't know how much other people noticed . . . but I felt like a totally new person . . . and I grew passionate about reading and memorizing God's Word."

Returning to North America in early 1982, Cole received a phone call from a church in Vancouver, asking him to come lead their worship. He accepted, and one day he noticed a cute Italian girl named Anna singing in the choir.

"I wasn't in a big hurry to start a relationship but . . . as I got to know Anna, I realized that she was meeting all of my nineteen prayer requests. It was time to get married. God was answering my prayer."

Mark and Anna were married in 1983, and now they tell their grandchildren the story of God's guidance on their lives.[5]

Remember how Nehemiah confessed his sin, reminded God of His promises, and prayed day and night? The Bible says, "The earnest prayer of a righteous person has great power and produces wonderful results" (James 5:16 NLT).

Prayer is the divine energy that brings the power of God into the plans He gives you, but you must learn to pray with fervor, persistence, and faith. I don't know any shortcut for this. God guides His children as they learn the joy of praying to Him night and day.

Practice Spontaneous Prayer

It's wonderful to have a leisurely hour on the patio for Bible study and prayer, or to engage in a special extended time in prayer with friends at church, beseeching God for His favors. But sometimes you have to pray instantly, urgently, on the spur of the moment. The Lord hears those prayers too!

I urge you to learn to pray quickly, silently, and instantly. No one in the Bible mastered that skill better than Nehemiah. His book is peppered with short prayers interjected into his narrative. He knew how to pray spontaneously.

For example, one day the king wanted a glass of wine, so Nehemiah prepared it: "I took the wine and gave it to the king. I had not been sad in his presence before, so the king asked me, 'Why does your face look so sad when you are not ill? This can be nothing but sadness of heart'" (Neh. 2:1–2 NIV).

Nehemiah knew those words could have reflected genuine concern, or they could have been his death sentence. It was a capital offense to be sad in the presence of Artaxerxes.

> I was very much afraid, but I said to the king, "May the king live forever! Why should my face not look sad when the city where my ancestors are buried lies in ruins, and its gates have been destroyed by fire?" The king said to me, "What is it you want?" Then I prayed to the God of heaven, and I answered the king, "If it pleases the king and if your servant has found favor in his sight, let him send me to the city in Judah where my ancestors are buried so that I can rebuild it." (Neh. 2:2–5 NIV)

I'm sure you noticed it—*then I prayed to the God of heaven, and I answered the king.*

In the twinkling of an eye, Nehemiah had his opportunity, but he had to say exactly the right words in the right way to move the king to his cause. His life was on the line, not to mention the desires of his heart. It was critical for him to speak wisely and for the king to react positively. So Nehemiah shot an arrow to heaven. Maybe it was just *"Help me, Lord!"*

And the Lord answered, and soon Nehemiah was on his way to rebuild the walls of Jerusalem (Neh. 2:6).

When you know how to earnestly pray day and night, you'll find there's also great power in spontaneous bursts of prayer. As one commentator put it, "Because Nehemiah was in the habit of praying regularly, his natural response to this dangerous situation was to offer up a quick, silent 'arrow prayer.'"[6]

One fateful day in 2001, Lt. Col. Dan Hooten was working on the first floor in the C ring of the Pentagon, which is in the middle of the building. He was preparing for a ten o'clock meeting when a coworker came into his office with news the World Trade Center was on fire in New York.

Hooten went to his boss's office, where the television was on. He watched the events unfold, then had a "feeling deep down" that he should get up and return to his own office. Along the way he stopped to talk to someone in a nearby cubicle. Suddenly the whole room burst into flames, and Hooten was thrown twenty feet forward. His left leg was pinned to the floor beneath rubble, and the walls were on fire. He yelled for his coworker but heard no response.

He recalls, "At that moment I said a short prayer, asking God to show me the way out."

Hooten pried his leg loose and saw some light in the distance. Crawling through an opening, he found he was trapped again. "The room was full of smoke, and so were my lungs. The room was like an oven, and at that moment I thought I was going to die of smoke inhalation."

Hooten climbed over more rubble and saw a hand stretching out to help him. All at once, he was on the helicopter pad outside the Pentagon. He began helping others, not realizing he was bleeding from multiple shrapnel wounds. When he shares his story now, he credits his survival to God's answering his simple words, "Show me the way out."[7]

Prepare for God to Do Things His Way

As God drops His seeds of inspiration into your mind and you pray over them—whether in quiet, extended prayer or in a quick, in-the-moment prayer—you'll learn to trust Him for His own brand of success. You have to expect Him to do things His way.

Proverbs 16:3 says, "Commit to the LORD whatever you do, and he will establish your plans" (NIV). The word *commit* means to "entrust." God can be trusted with your dreams—to divulge them, develop them, sometimes delay them, and always drench them with His blessings.

God opens and closes doors, arranges circumstances, and sometimes creates trajectories you didn't expect.

In Nehemiah's case, the king granted him letters of safe conduct through the empire, along with provisions for the walls and gates. Nehemiah said, "And because the gracious hand of my God was on me, the king granted my requests" (Neh. 2:8 NIV). Furthermore, Artaxerxes sent a military convoy to accompany him, because the Jews had strong enemies in the province of Judah.

Arriving in Jerusalem, Nehemiah wanted to keep his dream a secret until it was time to rally the Jews, so he saddled his horse in the darkness and inspected the ruins by moonlight. The next day he gathered the people and said, "'You see the trouble we are in: Jerusalem lies in ruins, and its gates have been burned with fire. Come, let us rebuild the wall of Jerusalem, and we will no longer be in disgrace.' I also told them about the gracious hand of my God on me" (Neh. 2:17–18 NIV). The people agreed and began working, and

Nehemiah declared with confidence, "The God of heaven will give us success" (Neh. 2:20 NIV).

I believe with all my heart the God of heaven will grant success to His sincere children who seek His will for their lives. But remember, success doesn't necessarily mean health, wealth, fame, and fortune. When God uses the term *success*, it means the fulfillment of His plan for you. And you have to trust Him however that unfolds if you want to move forward.

Many of you have listened to Susie Larson's friendly voice on the radio. In one of her books, Susie wrote about her husband, Kevin, who was a workaholic. He labored around the clock to provide for his family. Susie believed God could provide for them without Kevin working himself into the ground, and she began praying about it. She felt he was neglecting his family by working too hard. It became a deep burden to her.

"I took up my case before God with such resolve, I would not be denied," she said. "It's like I grabbed the horns of the altar and refused to let go. I couldn't help myself. If God didn't come through for us, I feared that our family life would fall *far* short of what God had promised us."

"Out on the limb I went. Facedown on the floor. I implored my God to move in my husband's heart and in his work situation. Each day I'd search Scripture for promises to anchor me, I'd cry out to the Holy Spirit for His presence to empower me, and I'd appeal to heaven for God to direct me."

As she continued her prayers, Kevin was diagnosed with a grave illness. Susie didn't see that coming, but she trusted God, saying, "I don't believe for a moment that God gave Kevin cancer to teach him a lesson, but I do believe God allowed something the enemy meant for evil, and He turned it for good in our lives."

As Kevin recovered, he realized the company he worked for had taken advantage of him. Another company in town was much better, but positions there were few and far between.

Susie kept the wires to heaven hot. "I prayed in the morning. I prayed in the evening. I prayed when I folded the clothes and when I prepared the kids' lunch."

One day, Kevin picked up the phone to hear the president of the other company with a job offer. "We could not have fathomed how God intended to use this breakthrough to change our lives," Susie wrote.[8]

Yes, you need to plan if you want to move forward toward God's plans for your life; but you also need to pray, for so much is out of your control. God doesn't always lead you as you expect, so you must improvise by faith.

The Bible says, "Now listen, you who say, 'Today or tomorrow we will go to this or that city, spend a year there, carry on business and make money.' Why, you do not even know what will happen tomorrow. What is your life? You are a mist that appears for a little while and then vanishes. Instead, you ought to say, 'If it is the Lord's will, we will live and do this or that'" (James 4:13–15 NIV).

That puts things in perspective, doesn't it? Commit to the Lord whatever you do with this attitude—*Lord, not my will but Yours be done.* The Lord Jesus has a wonderful way of fulfilling your plans beyond your expectations when you surrender your plans to Him. He is able to do "exceedingly abundantly above all that we ask or think, according to the power that works in us" (Eph. 3:20).

Plead for Overcoming Strength in Overwhelming Moments

As Kevin and Susie Larson learned, prayerfully following God's unfolding plan for your life means you may encounter tremendous obstacles, fears, and foes. Nehemiah learned that too.

Powerful forces in the province of Judah aligned against Nehemiah as soon as he showed up. The occupants of the land hated the presence of Jews in Jerusalem. One of the principle foes was a Samaritan war-lord named Sanballat. Modern research has shown him to be the commander of a garrison force, and he was a formidable opponent. Nehemiah 4 says:

> When Sanballat heard that we were rebuilding the wall, he became angry and was greatly incensed. He ridiculed the Jews, and in the presence of his associates and the army of Samaria, he said, "What are these feeble Jews doing? Will they restore their wall? Will they offer sacrifices? Will they finish in a day? Can they bring the stones back to life from those heaps of rubble—burned as they are?" (vv.1–2 NIV)

That's the situation Nehemiah faced—trying to recover stones for his wall from heaps of burnt rubble while taunted by enraged enemies.

You'll have opposition too. Like Sanballat, the devil will hurl his forces against God's unfolding work in your life. But don't be bullied. Don't be intimidated. Never let yourself stay discouraged. Do what Nehemiah did. Notice these two little verses that Nehemiah inserted into the story: "Hear us, our God, for we are despised. Turn their insults back on their own heads. Give them over as plunder in a land of captivity. Do not cover up their guilt or blot out their sins from your sight, for they have thrown insults in the face of the builders" (Neh. 4:4–5 NIV).

A few verses later—more problems, and more prayer!

"But we prayed to our God and posted a guard day and night to meet this threat" (Neh. 4:9 NIV).

A couple of chapters later—yet more problems, and yet more prayer!

"But I prayed, 'Now strengthen my hands'" (Neh. 6:9 NIV).

And so it goes. You must pray for strength in overwhelming moments. You need God to strengthen your hands as you go forward, and especially when you face unexpected or unwanted difficulties.

Karen Rhea was on a mission trip with her husband, Jim, a dentist.

Taking their seven-year-old son, Billy, with them, they went to the jungles of Mexico to provide volunteer dental care to remote villages. One stretch of the trip required riding mules along the mountain route with a local missionary and some villagers leading the way.

"My mule began to stumble his way up the steep incline," Karen wrote. "Rocks started to give way under his hooves. My saddle slid back toward his hindquarters."

Karen expected the animal to regain his footing, but instead he tumbled off the cliff. Karen separated from the mule in midair and landed with a sickening thud twenty-five feet below. Jim and the villagers scrambled down the side of the cliff; and when he lifted Karen's head, his hands were drenched with her blood.

To his intense relief, Karen opened her eyes. "Is the mule OK?" she asked. "What did I do wrong? I think my back is broken. Can we go home now?"

Karen was in shock, lapsing in and out of consciousness. Billy climbed down to be near his mom, his eyes filled with tears. That's when one of their companions raised his voice in prayer: "Father God, be with our sister, Karen. We know this situation grieves You as it does us. We beg You for added protection, aid, and healing. Give Jim and Billy comfort. Help us rely on Your life-sustaining, saving grace. Enable us all to do Your bidding. Guide us, we pray. Amen."

Dr. Rhea sent Billy and the others for help while he treated his wife's injuries with the medical supplies he'd brought for the villagers. He knew the area was infested with jaguars, and he felt their lives were on the line. But God answered his prayer! A party of villagers soon returned with a makeshift stretcher of balsa wood and vines.

"Though in shock," Karen says, "I recall the sensation of hands covering me head to toe." A Cessna aircraft carried them to a local hospital, and a week later Karen was able to fly home for a one-week stay in a trauma hospital, followed by six months of bed rest.

At one point during that time, she grew depressed, questioning "the enormity of the mistake I had made in going on the mission trip with Jim. Not only was my family traumatized, but we went to help others—yet our family became the ones in need."

Then a letter came from the jungle missionary. It seems the villagers felt enormously gratified as they became the hands and feet of Jesus. It gave them dignity and a sense of ministry. The joy they felt in rescuing Karen rallied and revived them. It had become a great blessing. Meanwhile, Karen recovered with nothing more than some occasional back pain, a story to tell, and a Savior to praise.

And, oh yes, in case you're wondering—the mule survived too![9]

Expect it: the devil will try to push you off the road. But the One to whom we pray is the One before whom devils tremble. God will give you overcoming strength for overwhelming moments.

That's what He did for Nehemiah. And get this—he and the residents of Jerusalem finished the wall in fifty-two days! Only God could have done that.

Believe me, you can't go forward in life without drenching every step in prayer.

One of the greatest ships of all time was the RMS *Mauretania*, built in 1906. It had a distinguished career, captured the world record for crossing the Atlantic, and served the British Navy during World War I. Even today, many of the furnishings of the *Mauretania* are woven into the interiors of some of the world's most exclusive buildings.

Hidden away in history is this interesting fact: "The *Mauretania* was built by prayer. The naval architect who constructed it would not put in a single piece of that great ship without definitely asking God to aid him, and he would not receive any part of the machinery without having the consciousness that it had also received the divine acceptance. Thus the greatest ship in the world has been built by making prayer a working-principle of life."[10]

Make prayer a working principle in your life by praying over every step you take. The only way to stay shipshape is to ask God for overcoming strength in overwhelming moments, and to go forward in His power. Remember, it's not your dream God wants—it's you!

Praise God for His Great Work in You

You have one more opportunity related to prayer as you move forward toward the future God has prepared for you. You have the privilege of praising God for His work in your life. Because Nehemiah and the Jews in Jerusalem finished the walls so quickly, they had some time on their hands. So what's next? How about a Bible conference?

With the security of a walled city, the Jewish settlers felt safe going about their lives. Furthermore, one section of the wall near the Water Gate formed a large new public square. So the word went out from there. All the people gathered in the Water Gate square, and Ezra the priest stood on a platform built for the occasion. He praised the God of heaven, and the crowd lifted their hands upward and shouted, "Amen! Amen!"

Ezra the scribe read directly from the Scriptures. He explained the meaning and gave the application. At first the people grieved, for they suddenly realized how much they had neglected God's Word. But Ezra and Nehemiah told them, "This day is holy to our Lord. Do not grieve, for the joy of the LORD is your strength" (Neh. 8:10 NIV).

The emotion of the crowd quickly changed, and the people rejoiced in what God had done.

Later, when the wall was dedicated, great choirs marched along the parapets, leading in worship. "And on that day they offered great sacrifices, rejoicing because God had given them great joy. The women and children also rejoiced. The sound of rejoicing in Jerusalem could be heard far away" (Neh. 12:43 NIV).

There's nothing like the joy of watching God form and fulfill His plan for your life. And it only happens as you step toward your dreams in His presence through prayer.

The great Christian humanitarian George Muller wrote, "The joy which answers to prayer give, cannot be described; and the impetus which they afford to the spiritual life is exceedingly great."[11]

Blogger Dionna Sanchez recalls a moment when God answered

a huge prayer for her family. A matter had weighed heavily on their hearts, and they had earnestly prayed about it. God answered unexpectedly, in His timing, and with perfect wisdom. So Dionna and her family decided to celebrate. They cracked open the sparkling cider and made a toast, raising their glasses into the air and saying, "Thank You, Lord, for answering our prayers."

She said, "I wanted my kids to understand that this wasn't just a 'good' thing that happened—it was a 'GOD' thing that happened!"

They danced around the kitchen, knowing things could have turned out very differently. "We were beyond thankful," she said. "We were overjoyed." It was a moment her family will long remember.[12]

That's how it was for the residents of Jerusalem as they rejoiced in their God, and their joy gave them renewed strength.

It will be that way for you too. So what's your next step?

I began this chapter by telling you about the inimitable Leonora Wood. Let me end with a special prayer composed by her daughter, Catherine Marshall. This prayer was inspired by her mother, and was included in Marshall's book *Adventures in Prayer*. Both Catherine and Leonora are in heaven now, but I'm sure they'd be thrilled if you make their prayer your own. Go ahead and read this part out loud if you want:

Father, once—it seems long ago now—I had such big dreams, so much anticipation of the future. Now no shimmering horizon beckons me; my days are lackluster. I see so little of lasting value in the daily round. Where is Your plan for my life, Father?

You have told us that without vision, we men perish. So Father in Heaven, knowing that I can ask in confidence what is Your expressed will to give me, I ask You to deposit in my mind and heart the particular dream, the special vision You have for my life.

And along with the dream, will You give me whatever graces, patience, and stamina it takes to see the dream through to fruition? I sense that this may involve adventures I have not bargained for. But I want to trust You enough to follow even if You lead along new paths. I admit to liking some of my ruts. But I know that habits that seem like cozy nests from the inside, from Your vantage point may be prison cells. Lord, if You have to break down any prisons of mine before I can see the stars and catch the vision, then Lord, begin the process now. In joyous expectation, Amen.[13]

Chapter 3

Choose

Diminish Your Distractions

Just months before America entered World War II, a young marine from Ohio named Walter Osipoff boarded a DC-2 transport plane. He and several other marines took off on a routine parachute jumping exercise as pilot Harry Johnson headed aloft into a beautiful blue San Diego sky.

Nine men jumped from the plane, then disaster struck. Osipoff was standing near the jump door when his rip cord caught on something and deployed. His chute flew open, and he shot from the plane like a rocket, hitting the side of the aircraft. The impact broke two of his ribs and fractured three vertebrae. As Osipoff plunged toward the ground he was yanked to a stop, then jerked backward. His parachute had wrapped around the plane's wheel, and the hapless marine found himself dangling fifteen feet below the plane's tail. He was literally hanging by a thread.

It got worse. The chute's chest strap and one leg harness had broken, so Osipoff was dangling in midair, upside down, suspended by a single strap which had slipped down to his ankle. His weight put tremendous pressure on the plane, and Johnson struggled to keep from nose-diving. Furthermore, Johnson had no radio contact, and the other men in the plane couldn't reach their buddy. The dangling marine, injured and terrified, kept his eyes squeezed shut against the rushing wind. Blood dripped from his helmet. He was stuck and facing certain death.[1]

I'll tell you the end of the story later, but for now I want you to imagine how helpless Walter Osipoff felt. You may not have dangled from an airplane, but have you ever felt like your life was turned upside down? Maybe you've felt like you were at the end of your rope, stretched to the breaking point, or stuck in a situation you couldn't escape. It's not usually as dramatic as what our marine friend experienced, but feeling powerless to change anything is real, and it can keep you frozen in place.

We've already seen the importance of prayer in our efforts to pursue our dreams. In this chapter, I want to show you how to diminish the distractions that bog you down and set the right priorities so that you can choose the best path forward.

Feeling Stuck?

Authors call it writer's block. Athletes call it a slump. Economists call it stagnation. Pastors call it burnout. Swimmers call it treading water. Off-roaders call it spinning their wheels. Retailers call it sluggishness. Scientists call it inertia. Retirees call it the "every day is Saturday" syndrome. Sailors call it the doldrums.

But I have good news. This is not God's intention for your life. The Bible says, "He who has begun a good work in you will complete it until the day of Jesus Christ" (Phil. 1:6).

You see, our mighty God has a plan for your life, and He doesn't intend to stop in mid-design! The One who composed the songs of the birds, fashioned the orbits of the planets, formed the cycles of history, and plotted the pathways of the great whales—that One has a unique design for your life. Nothing is more important than fulfilling it.

At certain points in life, you'll feel incapacitated and stuck, unable to gain forward momentum. Some of the greatest characters in the Bible were immobilized for a time:

- Moses was stuck on the backside of the desert for years, unaware of God's future for him (Ex. 3:1).
- Naomi was trapped in Moab after the deaths of her husband and sons (Ruth 1:5).
- Elijah was stuck in the wilderness, feeling sorry for himself after his failure to bring about the revival he'd hoped for Israel (1 Kings 19:10).
- Ezekiel was stranded in Babylon at age thirty, frustrated he couldn't enter his priestly service in Jerusalem at the temple (Ezek. 1:1).
- Peter was caught in a dark, depressive cycle on the Saturday before Easter (Matt. 26:75).
- Thomas was cast into faithless despondency when he missed the Savior's appearance on Easter Sunday (John 20:24).
- Paul was stuck in Troas where a great door of evangelism was open for him, but he had no peace of mind because of anxiety about problems in the Corinthian church (2 Cor. 2:12–13).
- The apostle John was exiled on the Island of Patmos, lonely and unable to continue his ministry—or so he thought (Rev. 1:9).

But wait! God has a design for every situation and every person. Look at that list again. By God's grace, each of these people managed to get themselves unstuck and they went forward, onto their greatest days of usefulness for the Lord.

You were created for an ever-fruitful, flourishing, thriving life.

Jesus said, "I have come that they may have life, and that they may have it more abundantly" (John 10:10). The Bible says, "Never be lacking in zeal, but keep your spiritual fervor, serving the Lord" (Rom. 12:11 NIV).

In 1 Corinthians 15:58, the apostle Paul proclaimed, "Therefore, my beloved brethren, be steadfast, immovable, always abounding in the work of the Lord, knowing that your labor is not in vain in the Lord."

You can't be stuck and live abundantly at the same time. You can't be despondent while keeping your spiritual fervor in God's service. You can't be immobilized and give yourself fully to the work of the Lord.

So how do you get free of the sandbar and back to sailing in open water?

Consider What's Best

Start by accepting the fact that everything is not equally important. Let me repeat that: everything in your life is not equally important. Almost every adult struggles with this today. We become so distracted by molehills that we can't charge up the mountain.

In February 2020, Dan Cain of Twinsburg, Ohio, came home to find postal workers hauling seventy-nine large bins of letters to his house. In one day he received fifty-five thousand letters, all of them the same. They were duplicate letters from a student loan company. Somehow the company made an error in its mailing system, inundating Cain with enough mail to last a lifetime.[2]

Now think of this. What if somewhere among those fifty-five thousand letters was a vital communication—a small package mixed among the bins? What if it was a letter from God? What if a small copy of the Bible, the message of hope and heaven, was jumbled among the letters in those seventy-nine bins of mail?

Your cluttered world bombards you with thousands of bits of data every day. No wonder you're distracted! It's easy for the most important things to be lost. That's why you must acknowledge that not everything is a priority. Not every activity is vital. Not every situation is eternal.

In His parable of the sower, Jesus said, "Now he who received seed among the thorns is he who hears the word, and the cares of this world and the deceitfulness of riches choke the word, and he becomes unfruitful" (Matt. 13:22).

Can you relate to that? I can. The Lord has sown the seed of His Word into our hearts, but it's not as productive or fruitful as He wants. Somehow His work in and through us is choked by "the cares of this world and the deceitfulness of riches."

Often times our inability to move forward is due to a lack of priorities—we fail to even consider that some things are more important than others. Without understanding the nature of priorities, you can't sort through the cares of this world, but you can become paralyzed by burdens, business, and busyness. In trying to do everything you end up doing nothing. This "paralysis by analysis" can devastate your morale and your emotional health.

In his book *Essentialism,* Greg McKeown wrote:

The word *priority* came into the English language in the 1400s. It was singular. It meant the very first or prior thing. It stayed singular for the next five hundred years. Only in the 1900s did we pluralize the term and start talking about priorities. Illogically, we reasoned that by changing the word we could bend reality. Somehow we would now be able to have multiple "first" things. People and companies routinely try to do just that. One leader told me of his experience in a company that talked of "Pri-1, Pri-2, Pri-3, Pri-4, and Pri-5." This gave the impression of many things being the priority but actually nothing was.[3]

Understanding that not all things are equally important is an essential part of the forward life. Priorities keep you focused and help you accomplish what really matters, because the best way forward is . . . forward!

Clarify What's Best

Once you've understood the significance of priorities, the next step to getting unstuck is to actually determine the *most important things* in your life. To do that you need the clarity to know what's best. Start by asking what's most important to God. What isn't as important to Him? What do you need to focus on in your life, and what can you start deleting?

Good authors know how to create an initial rough draft of their chapter, then read it and strip out unnecessary words—sometimes whole paragraphs. I've done that with this book; otherwise it would be twice the size. Good writing is like being a runner who sheds unnecessary clothing or a hiker who discards unneeded weight from his backpack.

To generate forward momentum, evaluate your activities. Delete things of less importance to keep things of greater worth. I can't give you an itemized list of what should be important to you. But in Mark 12, Jesus gave us three principles that should be central to everyone's life.

In that passage, a Jewish temple scribe approached Jesus asking advice on how to organize life. His specific question was, "Which is the first commandment of all?" (Mark 12:28).

The Great Commandment! The one above all others. The ultimate priority. In effect, the scribe was asking Jesus, "What is truly important in life? From God's perspective, what one thing is indispensable?"

This scribe came from a Jewish tradition boasting a multitude of commands and obligations. Jewish rabbis divided the Old Testament commandments into positive and negative laws and into major and minor laws. According to their calculations, the Old Testament contained 613 commandments. Of those, 248 tell us to do something positive and 365 prohibit us from doing something negative. This scribe was asking Jesus which of these 613 commandments was most important from God's perspective.

Jesus answered without hesitation: "The first of all the commandments is: 'Hear, O Israel, the LORD our God, the LORD is one. And you shall love the LORD your God with all your heart, with all your soul, with all your mind, and with all your strength.' This is the first commandment. And the second, like it, is this: 'You shall love your neighbor as yourself.' There is no other commandment greater than these" (Mark 12:29–31).

What an answer! Jesus boiled down the contents of the entire Old Testament into one overarching, overwhelming priority: love. And He ascribed to that priority three applications. Without understanding this, it's impossible to move forward. Love—as God defines love—is life's ultimate priority.

The Priority of Loving God

First is the priority of loving God. Quoting from Deuteronomy 6, Jesus said, "And you shall love the LORD your God with all your heart, with all your soul, with all your mind, and with all your strength" (Mark 12:30).

More than anything else, this is what we're made for—a passionate, practical embracing of God with all His attributes, all His virtues, all His grace, embracing Him with an overflowing heart of burning devotion and passionate enjoyment. That affects everything else we think, do, and say.

When actor Chris Pratt gave his acceptance speech at the Teen Choice Awards, he said, "I'm so thrilled to be here. . . . This means a lot to me. . . . I want to thank God. I always do that when I'm up on a platform in front of a bunch of young faces. I love God, that's my thing. I love Him! And you should too!"[4]

Like all of us, Pratt has ups and downs, but he's been increasingly vocal about Christianity, and he's not hesitant to tell teenage audiences that loving God should be a priority in their lives.

But what does it mean to love God?

In his book *Do I Love God?*, professor Rod Culbertson says the greatest question is: "Do you have emotions and passion for, and devotion to, the one living and true God, as well as a settled commitment that he is the Lord of your life and everything to you?"

Culbertson also asks, "What keeps you from loving God with a devoted, heartfelt love? Work, play, leisure, family, poor time management, technology, laziness, sin, or personal failure? The excuses and reasons are numerous and somehow allow us to ignore or underdevelop our relationship with God, the most important relationship in life. So, I conclude with one more question: 'Are you growing in your love for God?'"[5]

Elisabeth Elliot likewise said, "I have one desire now—to live a life of reckless abandon for the Lord, putting all my energy and strength into it."[6]

The Priority of Loving People

Jesus continued, "You shall love your neighbor as yourself" (Mark 12:31). Within the same priority of love there's a second application. We're to love our neighbors—and we have 7.7 billion of them! We can't know or personally care for each of them, but the Lord knows exactly how to lead us to those we need to serve.

Paul Lee, a police officer, spent years apprehending criminals and witnessing mind-numbing evils. He became so calloused that he said, "I felt nothing. I hated everybody. Nobody told you the truth."

Paul's marriage ended, and he descended into heavy drinking and constant cynicism. "I knew the life I was living . . . was passing before my eyes like a bad B-movie," he recalled.

Then his mother died. As he showered and prepared for her funeral, he thought of her dedication to Christ. "I knew the life I was living was totally wrong," he said. "I had faulted God for 20 years. But the death of my mother totally broke me and brought me to the lowest point in my life."

There under the steaming water of the shower, he said three things that his criminals often said to him: "I give up. I surrender. I throw in the towel." In an instant, he made Jesus the Lord of his life.

Shortly afterward, Paul joined the Fellowship of Christian Police Officers (FCPO). He felt a deep compassion for other cops suffering what he'd felt—"The feeling of aloneness and loneliness and that nobody really cares." Now he ministers to police officers in a way few can. He loves them as only a brother in blue can do.

"With a biblical mindset, you realize that God has put you there for His purposes, to carry out His mission, whatever that might be," Paul said.

Paul and his fellow members of the FCPO understand that Christian police officers are perfectly positioned to reach out to their colleagues and the public they serve. "We're on the mission field," he said. "You don't have to beat people over the head with the Bible. You just keep the compassion of Christ. Your purpose is far greater than just throwing somebody in jail."[7]

Loving others is sharing the compassion of Christ with the people around you.

The Bible says, "Owe no one anything except to love one another, for he who loves another has fulfilled the law. . . . Love does no harm to a neighbor; therefore love is the fulfillment of the law" (Rom. 13:8, 10). And the apostle Paul wrote, "For all the law is fulfilled in one word, even in this: 'You shall love your neighbor as yourself'" (Gal. 5:14).

As I was finishing this book, our world was rocked by the coronavirus pandemic. You know the details of the horrors and devastation caused by this plague. We're all living through it and have been affected by it.

As in all calamities and tragedies, we've had choices to make. The people of our congregation chose to use this pandemic as an opportunity to love our neighbors. With the leadership of David St. John, one of our senior staff members, we began providing food for people in our community. Each week we distributed over fifty thousand pounds of food. We fed one thousand families with basic food, living essentials, and a gallon of milk each. More than sixty of our fellow believers gathered every Friday, donned their masks and gloves, and put this gift of love in the trunks of cars as people in need drove through our campus.

Hundreds of emails, letters, and phone calls helped us realize what this meant to the recipients. Perhaps the greatest benefit of this initiative was the absolute, wild joy I witnessed in the lives of the people doing the giving. It truly is more blessed to give than to receive, and loving your neighbor is not something you feel . . . it's something you do!

For as James 2:8 says, "If you really fulfill the royal law according to the Scripture, 'You shall love your neighbor as yourself,' you do well."

But keeping priorities correctly aligned is a daily challenge. The first step is knowing what's at the top of the list. Once that's settled, other things fall into place more naturally. What comes first is clear: *love*—for God, for others, and then for ourselves.

The Priority of Loving Ourselves

Notice again how Jesus stated this command: "You shall love your neighbor *as yourself*" (Mark 12:31, emphasis added). That means it's okay to love ourselves. In fact, we are commanded to love ourselves!

Of course, we have to be careful at this point, because the devil always attempts to turn self-love into selfishness, ego, low and high self-esteem, conceit, haughtiness, self-importance, and all the other elements that make up sinful narcissism. I'm not recommending any of those things.

On the other hand, the apostle Paul said, "Therefore take heed to yourselves and to all the flock" (Acts 20:28).

Let me paraphrase here: take heed to yourselves and to everyone else assigned by God to your care.

If you don't take care of yourself, you can't take care of others. If you become fatigued and irritable, you can't uplift others. If you don't pay attention to your diet and exercise, you'll lose the strength you need to fulfill God's will.

You have a God-given responsibility to take care of yourself. Your body is the temple of the Holy Spirit. Your personality is the means by which God touches others. If you get in a rut, you'll pull others down into it with you. But when you have your priority—love—in its right place, and you understand its three applications, things have a way of moving forward.

Brad Hall wrote a newspaper column while his wife was expecting their baby boy. He wanted to convert the spare room into a nursery; but the room had become a sort of storage facility, so a lot of things had to be hauled out.

"While organizing for the nursery," he said, "I separated our items along the lines of priority and how often we might use them. The things we use regularly, I kept close by. The things we won't be using regularly were placed in the garage or deep in a closet. And everything else was either donated or placed in the yard sale pile."

Brad learned a lesson from that. "Our lives need to be organized so that God and our families can always come before everything else. Our jobs are important but they shouldn't come before God. Leisure time with loved ones is important but it also should not come before God. And if you have any sin in your life that is keeping you far away from God, you need to toss it out completely."

Brad concluded, "Put God ahead of everything else and he will take care of all of the rest."[8]

Amen! Sometimes our lives need to be cleaned out. A lot of our activities and attitudes should be jettisoned. Other interests need to be tucked away in an orderly place on our calendars. It's only possible to know what's worth keeping when you have the clarity to know what's best and when you understand the priority of love.

Choose What's Best

Once you have clarified what is God's best in your life, the next thing you need to do is actually choose those priorities. You need to make intentional, planned decisions that elevate what is best and remove what is merely good.

Doing so will require courage.

As Moses was dying, he told his successor, Joshua, "Be strong and of good courage, for you must go with this people to the land which the LORD has sworn to their fathers to give them, and you shall cause them to inherit it. And the LORD, He is the One who goes before you. He will be with you, He will not leave you nor forsake you; do not fear nor be dismayed" (Deut. 31:7–8).

It takes zero courage to stay in a rut. It takes grit and spunk to rouse yourself enough to climb out and move forward.

Every December our ministry, Turning Point, conducts a Christmas event in New York City on or near Broadway. As I walk down that street, I can't help noticing the glamorous theater marquees with the names of current plays on the Great White Way. It's a little like "déjà vu all over again," to quote Yogi Berra, because many of the plays are so-called "revivals."

The *New York Times* recently carried an article titled "Is Broadway Stuck on Replay?" about how Broadway producers are almost afraid to debut new shows, for the plays are unbelievably expensive to produce and apt to fail. So Broadway looks backward at past hits. People already know the music, and when they see the title on the marquee, a sense of nostalgia sets in. The *Times* writer said the current season on Broadway is beginning to "look like a rerun."[9]

Don't let your life be a rerun. Have the courage to do something new. Whatever God leads you to do, move forward. Once you establish your priorities, find the courage to say no to some things and yes to others. Let's look at two areas where this kind of courage is required.

Courage to Embrace Your Limitations

First, embrace your limitations. Do you have any of those? We all do! Beware of living in denial. To move forward you have to be realistic. Progress comes by embracing your God-given limits. Yes, I called them "God-given."

Some limits have to do with your age or stage in life. I used to do a lot of running for exercise, but now my knees won't allow it. So I have to accept that limitation and find other ways to get the exercise I need.

Some of your limitations have to do with the gifts God has given you or the location where He's placed you. Perhaps you're a faithful rural pastor. Your congregation will never be a so-called megachurch because of the region you're in. That doesn't mean you can't move forward to do great things for God. You can! He placed you there.

Perhaps you battle a handicap or a chronic illness, or you're a caregiver for someone who does. Maybe you have a dysfunctional family member, or you live in a dangerous area. You might be on a fixed income, or you couldn't afford to go to college, or your job is being phased out. Whatever they are, accept your limitations; don't use them as an excuse for not doing what God assigns you.

Even the Lord Jesus Christ had limitations. As almighty God, of course, He had no limitations. He was and is all-powerful, all-knowing, and all-loving. Not even the entire universe can contain Him. His power, might, grace, holiness, and justice are limitless, boundless, and measureless. But when the Son of God entered the human race in Bethlehem, He was confined within an animal's feeding trough. He grew up in a small hillside town. He did no recorded miracles for the first thirty years of His life, and He lived in submission to His parents.

When Jesus began His ministry, He didn't fly around like an angel from one preaching assignment to another. He didn't even have a horse or donkey, except on one known occasion. He said, "Foxes have holes and birds of the air have nests, but the Son of Man has nowhere to lay His head" (Matt. 8:20).

Jesus' area of ministry was limited to a little strip of land along the Mediterranean, and He never visited the great cities of His day: Athens, Rome, Milan, Alexandria, Carthage. He had a limited education, a limited income, and a limited time for His work—only about three years. Oh, and His nation wasn't free; it was occupied by Roman soldiers.

The limitless Son of God was financially, geographically, chronologically, politically, and physically limited. And then His limitations became far more stringent. On the cross, He became so limited by the nails in His hands and feet He was unable to wipe the blood from His eyes or scatter the flies from His face.

Yet His limitations worked for the advantage of the whole world. Imagine that! Limitations should never become excuses for staying where you are. Your priorities are determined by the gifts God has given you, your stage in life, and your personal shortcomings. Doesn't the Bible say something about God's strength being made perfect in our weaknesses (2 Cor. 12:9)?

Courage to Eliminate Your Distractions

To move forward, you need the courage to eliminate distractions by saying no to bad things and even saying no to some good things. You only want to say yes to the best things.

No to the bad. No to the good. Yes to the best!

Warren Buffett has learned he can't focus on too many things at once. He advises making a list of the top twenty-five things you want to accomplish in the next few years. From this list, pick the five that are most important to you. Now you have two lists. Buffett suggests you "avoid at all cost" the longer one, for those items may well prevent the big things from happening.[10]

To move forward in life, we have to discover the beauty of the word *no*. The practice of a graceful no takes courage, but boy, is it liberating!

On a bright winter day in California a few years ago, Greg McKeown visited his wife, Anna, in the hospital. Even in the hospital Anna was radiant. But she was also exhausted. It was the day after she had given birth to the couple's precious daughter—born healthy and happy at seven pounds, three ounces.

What should have been one of the happiest, most serene days of his life was actually filled with tension. Even as Greg's beautiful new baby lay in his wife's tired arms, he was on the phone and on e-mail with work, feeling the pressure to go to a client meeting. Greg's colleague had written to him, "Friday between 1–2 would be a bad time to have a baby because I need you to come be at this meeting."

Instinctively, Greg knew he should be with his wife and newborn child. But when asked whether he planned to attend the meeting, he said, "Yes."

"To my shame," Greg says, "while my wife lay in the hospital with our hours-old baby, I went to the meeting."

He was hoping the client would respect him for making that decision. But when he arrived, the look on the clients' faces mirrored how Greg felt. What was he doing there? Greg said yes simply to please; and in doing so he hurt his family, his integrity, and even the client relationship.

As it turned out, exactly nothing came of the client meeting. In trying to keep everyone happy, Greg sacrificed what mattered most and learned an important lesson in the process: if you don't set priorities in your own life, someone else will.[11]

In her book *Learning How to Say No When You Usually Say Yes*, Maritza Manresa advises her readers that it's all right to say no to lesser things to have room for the best things. Most of us say yes more than we should because we were taught to be available or because we don't want to disappoint others or challenge authority. Maybe we feel guilty, or we don't want to damage a relationship. As a result, we're constantly overcommitted, and the greater things are left behind.

Manresa suggests several ways to say no. The first is simply: "No!" That's a complete sentence. But if you want to be gentler about it, try statements like:

- I'm sorry, but I simply can't at this time.
- I have a personal policy . . .
- It doesn't look like I'll be able to, but if anything changes I'll let you know.

- It looks like I'm going to have to pass this time.
- I just can't fit it into my schedule.
- That is such a good cause, but I am already supporting other good causes.
- No, thank you.[12]

Is this hard for you? It is for me too. But we must have the courage to eliminate distractions if we're going to make forward progress.

Jesus often said no to others so that He could say yes to His Father. In Matthew 16, the Pharisees and Sadducees came to Jesus, asking Him for a sign. He said no. He gave them a blunt little sermon instead and left them and went away (Matt. 16:1–4). In Mark 1:38, Peter asked Jesus to return to Capernaum, where everyone wanted to hear Him. But Jesus said, "Let us go into the next towns, that I may preach there also, because for this purpose I have come forth."

We can't do everything, but we can always do our Father's will. We can fulfill His design for our days.

Commit to What's Best

Let me sum up where we've been in this chapter. When you get stuck, find some traction to give you forward momentum. God doesn't want you spinning your wheels. Once you're moving, you need clarity to know what direction to move in, and Jesus provided that by telling you to love God, love those around you, and love yourself. Armed with that clarity, you need the courage to say no to some things so you can say yes to the best things. And finally, you need the consistency to practice what's best. Proverbs 23:17 says, "But be zealous for the fear of the LORD all the day."

Paul said that we are to be "His own special people, zealous for good works" (Titus 2:14).

When you do what I've suggested in this chapter, you'll place yourself in the paths God has promised to bless. Even when things appear discouraging, keep pressing ahead, trusting God to make a way. Stay committed to what's best, for the Lord takes things from there and works wonders.

I entered the ministry over fifty years ago at a start-up church in Fort Wayne, Indiana. And I was focused. Man, was I focused! I wasn't necessarily aiming to be a spiritual success; I just didn't want to be a miserable failure.

All my friends knew I went to Fort Wayne to start a church. I wanted to prove to them and to myself that I could build a church from scratch. So I was knocking on doors every spare moment—all day Saturday and Sunday, in the afternoon, at night. I was gone all the time. I was doing the work of God! What could be better?

But at that time, my wife, Donna, and I had two little children. Jan was a toddler and David was just thirteen months younger. While Donna was at home with our kids, I was out on my white horse, winning people to Jesus and building the church. When I came home for dinner each day, Donna would say to me, "Are you going to be gone again tonight?" I was struggling to balance my responsibilities to my family and to the ministry. And then I'd go out and knock on some more doors, only to come home to the hurt look on my wife's face. I thought I was doing God's will; but really, I was doing David's will. I just didn't want to fail.

One day, Donna sat me down in the kitchen and said, "Honey, I just want to tell you I am never going to ask you again, 'Are you going to be gone tonight?' I've been thinking and praying about this, and the fact is, you are the priest in this family, and one day you're going to have to stand before God and give account of how you led us. If you believe God wants you to lead us by being gone all the time, then I'm not going to argue with you. This is all in your lap now. You are responsible."

That was a turning point in my life. I realized there are no ultimate conflicts in God's perfect will. He doesn't call a man to be both a father and a pastor in such a way that those two roles constantly war against each other. I began to pray God's priorities back into my life. Soon they became crystal clear to me. I organized them into the following four statements:

- I am a person with a responsibility before God.
- I am a partner with a responsibility to my wife.
- I am a parent with a responsibility to my kids.
- I am a pastor with a responsibility to my congregation.[13]

I haven't always lived up to these four priorities, but whenever I find myself straying, I feel these principles pulling me back into line. That's what priorities do!

My four children are grown now and I have twelve grandchildren. The priority lesson that God taught me is being lived out now in the way my children are parenting my grandchildren. I see it almost every day and I smile.

Grab on to God's Priorities

And that brings us back to our marine. Sorry to leave the story . . . well, dangling. But you know, those marines have a motto—*Semper Fi*—always faithful. They're not people who easily give up.

Walter Osipoff was hanging by his ankle, pulled behind a plane by the cords of his parachute, which were entangled in the plane's wheels. The pilot, Harold Johnson, was running out of fuel, but he knew an emergency landing would kill Walter.

Johnson descended to about three hundred feet above the ground and started circling the air base. Most people who saw the plane thought it was towing some piece of equipment. But one pilot—Lt. Bill Lowrey—glanced up and instantly knew what was happening. Spotting a nearby marine, John McCants, Lowrey shouted, "There's a man hanging on that line!" The two jumped into an SOC-1, a two-seat, open-cockpit plane, and they took off without even knowing if the aircraft was fueled.

Suddenly everyone on the ground realized the nature of the emergency, and every eye was transfixed. There were no radios on the planes, but Lowrey hand-signaled Johnson to head toward the Pacific, and the two planes rose to an altitude of three thousand feet. The SOC-1 maneuvered beneath the larger plane, and McCants stood upright in his rear cockpit seat and lunged for Osipoff. Grabbing him by the waist, he pulled him across the tiny seat. But Osipoff was still attached to the harness.

Now both planes and all the marines were in mortal danger.

Somehow—it was the grace of God—Lowrey inched his plane closer and closer to the DC-2 and actually bumped it, but in the process the propeller sliced through the remaining cords of Osipoff's parachute and freed him.

After flying through the air for more than half an hour dangling on a parachute line, Osipoff was free but not yet safe. Now the cut parachute cord became entangled in the SOC-1's rudder, and Lowrey struggled to maintain control of the plane. But he did—and when he landed, a roaring shout came from the crowd. They'd just witnessed what was later called "one of the most brilliant and daring rescues in naval history."

And as for our hapless marine, Walter Osipoff, he spent six months in the hospital. As soon as he recovered he went right back to work—jumping out of airplanes.[14]

Good for him!

You've been hanging around long enough. Grab on to the lifeline of God's priorities, and move forward in His design for your life, always abounding with His momentum and with His blessings!

Chapter 4

Focus

Make Your One Thing the Main Thing

The Maestro was born in the northern Italian city of Modena. His mother was a cigar factory worker, his father was a baker and amateur tenor. It was the amateur tenor part that most touched young Luciano Pavarotti. He loved hearing his dad sing, and he spent hours listening to the family's collection of recordings of great tenors. Father and son sang along with the records at full volume. Mr. Pavarotti wouldn't sing in public due to stage fright, but he did sing in the church choir. At age nine, Luciano joined him. The boy loved to sing—and people loved hearing him.

"Your voice touches me whenever you sing," his mother said.

But the question of a career was vexing. In those days just after World War II, a musical career was risky. His mother suggested Luciano become an athletic instructor, while his father encouraged him to continue developing his voice. "But you will have to study very hard, Luciano," he said. "Practice harder, and then maybe."

Luciano continued his musical studies and also enrolled in a teacher's college. After graduation, he asked his father, "Shall I be a teacher or a singer?"

The older man wisely avoided giving a direct answer. Instead he spoke words his son never forgot: "Luciano, if you try to sit on two chairs, you will fall between them. For life, you must choose one chair."

Luciano chose singing. It took seven years of hard study and intense practice before he made his first professional appearance, and it took another seven before he reached the Metropolitan Opera.

But Pavarotti lived with a single focus. Ultimately, he became one of the most famous operatic singers in the world—the King of High Cs, and a crossover performer who won the admiration of millions who had never set foot in an opera house. His final performance was viewed by the entire world as he sang "Nessun Dorma" at the 2006 Winter Olympics in Turin.

"I was blessed with a good voice by God," Pavarotti said. "I think it pleased Him that I decided to devote myself to it. And now I think whether it's laying bricks, driving a straight nail, writing a book, whatever we choose we should give ourselves to it. Commitment, that's the key. Choose one chair."[1]

Like Pavarotti, you have been blessed by God. You've been blessed with talents, resources, and a dream for the next phase of your life. Once you've prayed about that dream and set the right priorities to achieve it, your next step is to focus your life on that one main thing.

The Focus of My Life

I, too, had a father who knew how to pass along wise counsel at the right time. When I finished my seminary training many years ago, my father preached the sermon at my ordination ceremony. He based it on a passage in Acts 13, "David . . . served his own generation by the will of God" (v. 36). Of course, this was written about King David, but that is who I am named for. That day my father challenged me.

I have never forgotten his challenge. It's been a touchstone for me, a vision. More than once it helped me focus and pray, "God, that's what I want to do. I want to serve my generation by Your will."

I can't serve the generation that's past. They are gone. I can't serve the generation that's just starting; I probably won't be here to do that. But God has given me this little window of opportunity to serve my generation, and by His grace I want to stay focused on that.

There have been times I've been distracted and times when I felt like I was being destroyed, times when I was discouraged and disappointed and even felt defeated.

But here's what I've learned: when those things start happening, it's because you've lost your focus. When I start feeling those emotions, I have to shut down and get away some place with my Bible, my notebook, and my journal. I have to back away from all the pressure and say, "Lord, I'm starting to feel things I shouldn't feel if I stay focused. Now help me to get focused again."

Do you ever do that? "Lord, help me to focus on Your will for my life so I won't be distracted, destroyed, discouraged, disappointed, or defeated." When I do that, I have victory in my soul, and so will you. It is my wish for you that you will know God in such a way that you are absolutely certain what His purpose is for your life.

In the Bible, the apostle Paul had that kind of focus. He said he was straining forward, pressing on to reach a heavenly treasure. He wrote to his friends in the city of Philippi, saying:

> Not that I have already attained, or am already perfected; but I press on, that I may lay hold of that for which Christ Jesus has also laid hold of me. Brethren, I do not count myself to have apprehended; but one thing I do, forgetting those things which are behind and reaching forward to those things which are ahead, I press toward the goal for the prize of the upward call of God in Christ Jesus. (Phil. 3:12–14)

Paul was writing to a church for whom he had literally shed his blood. When he began preaching in the city of Philippi as recorded in Acts 16, he attracted both converts and critics. The critics seized him, stripped him, and whipped him until the blood ran down his back. He and his fellow sufferer, Silas, were cast into prison. But the church was worth the beating, becoming endeared to Paul and sending him financial help again and again. The church prayed for him as he traveled the empire. It was to these beloved people that Paul openly expressed the deepest longing of his heart and revealed his personal mission statement—the focus of his life.

As we unpack Paul's words, I want to show you four powerful principles that will sharpen your focus and guide you forward toward your next steps in life.

Focus on God's Purpose

Bob Weighton celebrated his 112th birthday during the coronavirus outbreak in 2020, which meant he wasn't able to have a party or be with friends. That's a shame, because on that day Bob became the oldest living man on earth. The Guinness World Records organization sent him a certificate, and newspapers hailed him in heroic terms. Friends sang "Happy Birthday" from a distance while Weighton, a former missionary school teacher, listened on his balcony.

"I can't say I am pleased to hear that the previous holder has died, but I am very pleased that I've been able to live so long and make so many friends," he said.

When asked about the virus, he said, "It's bizarre. I've never experienced anything like coronavirus before. I'm a bit frustrated, but then again I've been in situations where you just had to accept what was happening."

Then he summed up the wisdom of a 112-year-old: "There is

nothing we can do about it so you might as well do what you can. Never mind about the things that you can't."[2]

That's the key! Focus on what you *can* do. There's plenty you can't do, but there's one thing we can all do: we can follow God's deep desire for us to grow into the image of Jesus Christ. Paul said, "I press on, that I may lay hold of that for which Christ Jesus has also laid hold of me" (Phil. 3:12).

That is God's ultimate purpose for you and for all of us. Of course, He also has an individual plan for your life and for mine, and I'll deal with that in a moment. But first, consider God's ultimate purpose for your life—that you become more and more like His Son, Jesus Christ. Romans 8:29 says: "For whom He foreknew, He also predestined to be conformed to the image of His Son."

John Bray was Dean of Chapel at Indiana Wesleyan University. He and his wife were popular with students, and his chapel messages were full of life and truth. Then Bray was diagnosed with Parkinson's disease. The onset of symptoms led him to resign his position, but he simply continued looking ahead. He continued moving forward.

"Everybody gets a diagnosis of some kind sometime in their life," Bray told the campus newspaper. "There's no reason I shouldn't."

He told his students he is not asking why. "I can't change what's happened to me, so *why* is not a pivotal question in my life. Now, 'how will I glorify God in the midst of all this?' that's at the heart of almost every major decision a Christ-follower needs to make."

Speaking of his disability, Bray said, "Even this, that I don't like, is designed to shape me more like Christ."[3]

That is the voice of someone who has grasped onto God's purpose for his life, and no matter what comes at him, he will not let go.

Matt Mooney is a professional basketball player who, like every athlete, tries to excel at his sport, with its victories and setbacks. He's also a dedicated follower of Jesus. "I know God has a great plan for me. I trust in him. His purpose for me is to glorify him playing the game."

He said, "I can't take the game of basketball with me to eternity. The only thing that is eternal is God and Jesus. I realized that years ago. When I started really focusing on my faith, I realized no matter how I played, good or bad, God still loved me and I still had my salvation intact."[4]

Pastor Rick Warren wrote, "Your spiritual transformation in developing the character of Jesus will take the rest of your life, and even then it won't be completed here on earth. It will only be finished when you get to Heaven or when Jesus returns."[5]

When God looks at you and evaluates you, He wants you to become more and more like Jesus Christ, to follow Him closely and to emulate His life so that Christ is seen in you more and more. That only happens as you put your focus on Him.

Focus on God's Perspective

Next, Paul talked about seeing life through God's eyes. He briefly spoke about his past and said it wasn't worth focusing on: "Brethren, I do not count myself to have apprehended; but one thing I do, forgetting those things which are behind" (Phil. 3:13).

In 1954, Roger Bannister was a medical student who enjoyed running. He entered a race in Oxford on May 6 of that year and made history, becoming the first athlete to run a mile in less than four minutes. Bannister's time was 3 minutes, 59.4 seconds. Half a globe away, Bannister's rival, John Landy of Australia, took notice. A month later, Landy beat Bannister's record by about a second.

The media turned their spotlights on the two runners, and thousands of people watched later that summer when they lined up at the British Empire Games in Vancouver, Canada. It was called the "Mile of the Century." The racers shot from the starting blocks and Landy took the lead, which he maintained. The roar of the crowd was deafening. With only ninety yards to go, Landy made a fatal mistake. He glanced behind him. At that exact moment, Bannister streaked by him and won the race by less than a second.

The race became known as the Miracle Mile, and a Vancouver sculptor created a bronze statue of the two men at the moment when Landy glanced back. Landy later said, "Lot's wife was turned into a pillar of salt for looking back. I am probably the only one ever turned into bronze for looking back."[6]

The apostle Paul would have loved that story because that's what he was talking about in Philippians 3. He spoke of "forgetting" the things that are behind us, using the word *forget* in the sense of minimizing the negative impact of our past. Stop allowing things from the past to control you in the present or hinder you in the future. Paul shook things off. He didn't let them cling to him like anchors pulling him down.

Forget Your Past Successes

Here was the great apostle who accomplished more in his lifetime than most of us could accomplish in ten lifetimes, and he said, in effect, "I have not yet arrived." That amazes me, because I've spent my lifetime studying Paul's life and writing, and his influence for Christ is breathtaking.

N. T. Wright wrote about the impact of the apostle's letters, saying:

Paul's letters, in a standard modern translation, occupy fewer than eighty pages. . . . It is safe to say that these letters, page for page, have generated more comment, more sermons and more seminars, more monographs and dissertations than any other writings from the ancient world. . . . It is as though eight or ten small paintings by an obscure artist were to become more sought after, more studied and copied, more highly valued than all the Rembrandts and Titians and all the Monets and Van Goghs in the world.[7]

Paul's epistles comprise only part of his ministry. He also founded most of the churches in Asia Minor and was an intellectual giant.

Some consider him the greatest man who ever lived, apart from Jesus Christ. Yet here he was in the twilight of his life, looking back and saying, "I'm not there yet. I haven't apprehended the spiritual quality of life I want for myself. I've not yet been perfected. I'm going to continue to strive for that which God has called me."

One scholar observed, "Paul did not keep turning over in his mind the good old days of active service before he was imprisoned; he did not constantly remind himself of all his achievements nor continually recount those special high points of his intimate relationship with Christ. . . . He is not distracted by all the trophies of the past."[8]

Forget Your Past Mistakes

The other way of taking God's perspective regarding your past is to simply make up your mind to forget those things that haunt you. As Ruth Bell Graham quipped, "Every cat knows some things need to be buried."

The founder of the Red Cross, Clara Barton, was once offended by a coworker, but she quickly forgave her friend and went on. Years later, someone reminded her of the incident and said, "Don't you remember?"

"No," replied Miss Barton. "I distinctly recall forgetting that."[9]

There need to be things in your life that you distinctly recall forgetting. What things in your past could you choose to forget? For example, guilt is remembering a sin that's already been buried by the blood of Christ. Bitterness is remembering an offense that should be buried by grace. Discouragement is letting the last setback become a roadblock.

Your brain wants to relive events over and over. If you let it, it will haunt you with failures, shame you with mistakes, keep you awake with stress, and lull you to sleep with nostalgia. You can override your brain by giving the past to God and then "forgetting" the things that would pull you back and down.

If you know Christ as Savior, there's absolutely no reason to obsess over past failures. The blood of Christ frees you from beating yourself up with regrets. When you become a follower of Christ, you enter into a new life in Him, and your past is put behind you once and for all. Satan loves to remind you of your history with all its failure, but that's when you say with Jesus, "Get behind me, Satan!"

Remember, Paul had a wicked past. He cruelly persecuted Christians and attacked the church. He helped condemn Stephen— the first Christian to be martyred for the cause of Christ. After Paul's dramatic conversion on the Damascus Road, many Christians were still afraid of him.

What if Paul had continued to live in that past? What if he kept flogging himself for what he'd done? He would have lost his influence. Instead, he acknowledged his past but was full of gratitude to God for the grace of total forgiveness.

Harry J. Kazianis is Senior Director of Korean Studies at the Center for the National Interest in Washington and an expert on issues of foreign affairs. Seeing his success today, you'd never know that starting in the seventh grade Kazianis was constantly bullied. "The worst of the bullies was a kid named Joe. I can still see his face— and the grin he would flash at me—before it would begin. Joe would call me the worst things you can think of . . . words that aren't suitable for print. Soon, his verbal lashings became physical. He would punch me in the arms and legs to start. It then escalated to daily, full-body beatings where two or three of his friends would jump in."

Kazianis was paralyzed by these beatings, too afraid to fight back. He hid at school. He ate his lunch in the bathroom stall. Other kids piled on, and the next several years for Kazianis were torment.

"All of this left me an emotional mess for years," he said.

When Kazianis went to college, he was afraid to make friends. When a professor offered feedback, he felt attacked. He wanted to study national security issues and dreamed of speaking on foreign policy, but he had no ability to manage one-on-one situations in which conversations became intense. Even mild criticism felt like bullying.

As a result, Kazianis gave up his dream and got a job in sales. But during the 2008 financial crisis, when his income dramatically dropped, he lost his coping mechanism for pain and fell into a deep depression. He sat down with his wife and started crying uncontrollably. He told her what had happened years before, and a flood of pent-up anger and grief was released.

Harry's wife is a therapist, and she worked with him patiently and persistently, helping him make peace with the past and, in a clinical sense, forget what was behind and press forward. Kazianis learned to look at his past in a new way. He realized there were depths of understanding that came from his experiences. He learned that the past should never overwhelm the future, but it can inform it.

Kazianis went back to college and achieved his dream career. Now he offers international insight in Washington, DC, working just steps from the White House.

"But it almost didn't happen," he wrote. "I nearly let the past destroy my future."[10]

I've been a pastor for a long time, and I've noticed that many of God's people get stranded in the past. Some get stuck on their successes and rest on their laurels. Some are left high and dry by their failures, and a sort of post-traumatic fear grips their hearts.

Has that happened to you? Be honest, now. You must glance back, learn the lessons of the past, and celebrate your successes with humility. But it's one thing to glance back; it's another to get marooned in your memories.

The past lends perspective for the future. But if you linger there too long, your recollections will obliterate your dreams and hinder you from going forward.

Focus on God's Plan

As we continue with our passage in Philippians, notice that Paul became more specific, moving from our perspective to our plans—"Reaching forward to those things which are ahead" (Phil. 3:13).

God's purpose for all of us is the same—to become more like Jesus. But His plans for each of us are unique. He has a distinct blueprint for the life of every individual on earth and in history. His plan for you is tailor-made for you and you alone. It's perfect for the way He made you and the experiences you've had. Everything has prepared you for His next step in your life. But you have to follow Him into unknown territory—into the future. It's a walk of faith.

Tony Bombacino is the cofounder of a company that makes 100-percent real-food meals for people who must be fed with a tube. He and his wife have two children, including a special-needs child named AJ. He is tube-fed, nonverbal, and suffers from brain malformations and epilepsy.

"On August 31, 2011, my life changed forever," Tony wrote in a blog. "This is the day my otherwise thought-to-be-healthy 6-month-old son, AJ, had a 45-minute seizure out of the clear blue. The next week was filled with both moments I wouldn't wish on my worst enemy and moments of clarity that brought my wife and I closer together than ever before."

Tony wrote that, though he didn't realize it at the time, key experiences in his past had prepared him to be a special-needs dad. He grew up poor, which made him appreciate the smallest of blessings. He was a lifelong athlete, which provided incredible mentors through good coaching. He received a basketball scholarship, and college life taught him the need for extreme time management. He lost his mom as a teenager, which showed him the value of relationships. And he lost his older brother and best friend, Scott, to cancer in 2009, which has provided enduring inspiration.

"I draw tremendous strength from all he taught me before and during his final battle. He was always so humble, so appreciative of the little things and so present for the most important things. . . . In the moments when I feel like everything is falling apart, where I feel like I can't go on, where I feel afraid and unprepared and where I just want to break down—I remember Scott's example of courage, mental toughness, and always finding the good even in the worst situations."

"As a Special Needs Dad," Tony wrote, "I draw on these lessons and memories every day."[11]

If an American father and businessman can build on his past experiences and see how they fit into a plan for his life, so can we as we trust God's guiding hand.

Psalm 37:23 says, "The steps of a good man are ordered by the LORD, and He delights in his way." We aren't good in ourselves, but we are good in Christ. And in Christ, God not only orders your steps and your stops, He delights in the way He guides you forward. If He delights in His plans for you, shouldn't you delight in them too?

Focus on God's Prize

Finally, to live a focused life, fix your attention on heaven and the reward that awaits you there. Paul wrote: "I press toward the goal for the prize of the upward call of God in Christ Jesus" (Phil. 3:14).

For Paul, the goal and the prize were one and the same. Though not defined in this verse, this is a clear reference to the many promises given to those who are victorious in Christ, including a word of commendation from the Lord Jesus: "Well done, good and faithful servant" (Matt. 25:21). It embraces "the crown of righteousness" (2 Tim. 4:8). I could also refer to what Peter called the "crown of glory that does not fade away" (1 Pet. 5:4). Whatever else, this prize and goal will be more than eye has seen or ear has heard or man has ever contemplated (1 Cor. 2:9).[12]

Remember, Paul was using the metaphor of an Olympic race. In the ancient Olympics, if a runner won his race, he was summoned from the stadium floor to the judge's box where a wreath of laurel was placed on his head. He received financial rewards and some great fringe benefits: his food was provided for the rest of his life, and he had lifelong tickets on the front row of the Athenian theater.

But all those runners have been dead for centuries. Their prizes came to an end, their glory evaporated, the food lost its savor, and the Athenian theater is now in ruins. It was all temporary.

The prize of the upward calling of God in Christ Jesus is eternal! According to the apostle Peter, you have "an inheritance incorruptible and undefiled that does not fade away, reserved in heaven for you" (1 Pet. 1:4).

Keeping your eyes focused on the prize is the motivation that keeps you going, as Florence Chadwick learned. Chadwick was an accomplished long-distance swimmer and the first woman to swim the English Channel in both directions, setting new records each way. In 1952, thirty-four-year-old Florence set out to break another record. No woman had yet swum the twenty mile channel between Catalina Island and the California coast.

The conditions on the morning of her swim were not ideal. The water was cold and fog had settled in. Soon after she began to swim she could barely see the boats accompanying her. To make matters worse, sharks trailed her several times and had to be driven off.

Still, Florence swam on for more than fifteen hours as the fog grew increasingly dense and opaque. Finally, physically and emotionally exhausted, she stopped swimming. She was pulled into the boat and taken toward the California shore—which she discovered to her dismay was little more than a half-mile away. After swimming almost twenty miles, she had quit just barely short of her goal.

On the following day she told the news media, "All I could see was the fog. . . . I think if I could have seen the shore, I would have made it."

Two months later, Florence was back on Catalina Island, stepping into the water to try the swim again. Unfortunately, weather conditions were no better. The water was cold, and again, a dense fog settled over the channel. But this time she swam all the way, the first woman to make it. What made the difference? She later said that while swimming those last grueling miles, she kept her mind focused on a vivid mental image of the California shore. "At that moment," she said, "I knew the real meaning of faith described in the Bible as, 'the substance of things hoped for; the evidence of things not seen.'"[13]

Focus on Your One Thing

This, then, is the four-lane road God wants you to focus on as you move forward in life: driving down the lanes of His purpose, His perspective, His plan, and His prize for you. But there's one final thing that draws all this together as you seek to move forward toward God's plan for the next phase of your life: you must find your passion and give your life to *one thing*. You must choose one chair. As an old Russian proverb put it, "If you chase two rabbits, you'll not catch either one."

Gilbert Tuhabonye is one of the best runners in the world—a skill he developed when he had to literally run for his life as a boy in Burundi.

His story is harrowing. In October 1993, Gilbert was sitting in his high school class, probably thinking about running. He'd developed a love for track-and-field events in junior high, and he could hardly wait to tear around the track again.

But that day, the simple routines of the classroom were shattered by Hutu terrorists. The school was invaded by hostile members of the tribe, who descended on the children with genocidal rage. More than a hundred Tutsi children and their teachers were forced into a small room and hacked to death with machetes or burned alive. Gilbert wasn't killed, but he found himself at the bottom of a pile, buried under the burning corpses of his classmates.

The smoldering fire ate into Gilbert's skin, but he remained hidden for more than nine hours while the torturers stayed outside laughing and dancing. Finally, Gilbert smashed through a window and took off like an arrow. The Hutus chased him, but Gilbert outran them and made it to a local hospital, where doctors told him he would never run again.

Gilbert didn't believe the doctors. He felt God had spared him and that the Lord had a plan for his life. "I always knew that my faith would be tested, and it certainly was in those hours when my school was attacked. My belief in God never faltered. I never blamed Him or wondered how He could have let such a thing happen to me or to my classmates and teachers. I accepted what was taking place and knew that it was all part of a plan much larger than me."

Gilbert persevered until he was running well enough to win the Burundi National Championship in the 400 and 800 meters. His coaches felt he had Olympic potential, and he was sent to the United States as part of an Olympic training program. There, Abilene Christian University offered him a scholarship.

After graduation, Gilbert moved to Austin to coach young runners, and soon his ministry was off and running. His books, speeches, and coaching have touched thousands of lives. What's more, Gilbert started the Gazelle Foundation, whose slogan is "Run for the Water," to fund and build clean water projects for the people of Burundi. His "Gilbert's Gazelles" training group provides motivation and help to runners of all ages at all levels.[14]

I like someone like that—someone who never loses focus, who runs to win, whose life is defined by one thing. You see this kind of focus often in the Bible, because the writers of the Bible knew something about focusing on one thing.

David said, "One thing I have desired of the LORD, that will I seek: that I may dwell in the house of the LORD all the days of my life, to behold the beauty of the LORD" (Ps. 27:4).

Jesus said to the rich young ruler, "One thing you lack: Go your way, sell whatever you have and give to the poor, and you will have treasure in heaven; and come, take up the cross, and follow Me" (Mark 10:21).

He told the distracted homemaker, Martha: "One thing is needed, and Mary has chosen that good part" (Luke 10:42).

The man healed by Jesus said, "One thing I know: that though I was blind, now I see" (John 9:25).

And the apostle Paul said, "I focus on this one thing" (Phil. 3:13 NLT). The phrase *one thing* implies *consecration*—a word meaning to dedicate yourself and your every day to the wonderful will of God.

At the core of Paul's life was one motivating principle: he focused on Christ. He concentrated on his walk with Jesus. He said, in effect, "Lord, Your will be done—today and every remaining day I have on this earth. Not my will, but Yours be done!"

Kent Hughes wrote,

> Single-mindedness, the ability to focus, to shut everything out when necessary is the key to success in virtually every area of life. It is the essential ingredient of the manic virtue of basketball heroes Michael Jordan and Tim Duncan, or of golf great Jack Nicklaus or the creative musical genius of Wolfgang Amadeus Mozart.
>
> But here the focus is not a basketball rim, a flag fluttering on a distant green or a musical score—it is Christ Himself and how to please Him. The single-minded disciple is in the world but he does not get "entangled" in the world. He avoids anything that will hinder single-minded dedication to his Master.[15]

And that brings me to the secret of the focused life: staying committed to your passion . . . to your *one thing*. Several years ago I was reminded of this truth when I was invited to tour one of the largest carrot farms in America. Our host showed me the countless ways carrots are consumed: carrot juice, carrot cake, baby carrots, and dozens of other products I never dreamed came from carrots. When I asked, "How much of the carrot do you use?" our host replied: "We use every part of the carrot! Not a single bit goes to waste."

To illustrate his point, he went to the whiteboard and sketched a carrot. He then carefully labeled every part of the carrot and how it's used. And he was right—nothing goes to waste!

My friend built a hugely successful business by staying totally focused on carrots.

When I returned to my office, I gathered our staff together and told them about my whiteboard lesson on carrots. Then I went to our whiteboard and rough-sketched a Bible and said: "This is my carrot! Let's stay focused on our one thing!"

Together, we renewed our commitment to exclusively focus the ministry of Turning Point on the Bible and to deliver the Word of God in as many creative ways as possible. We thought of all the things we do that are based squarely on the Word of God: Sunday sermons, radio and TV programs, internet streaming, other social media, magazines, books, DVD albums, CD albums, study guides, E-devotionals, multi-language translations, and a host of other products and channels under the umbrella of Turning Point Ministries. Our goal is like that of my carrot-farming friend: let nothing of the pure and precious life-giving Word of God be wasted! Let us be good stewards of the calling God has given us to proclaim His Word to as many people as possible in our lifetime and beyond!

This is our mission. This is our one thing. This is our focus!

I don't know the details of God's plan for your life, but I do know this: as you focus on His purpose, His perspective, His plan, and His prize, He will guide you on the journey forward. Commit yourself to following the Lord to the best of your ability, and soon you will enjoy the adventure of discovering and living for your one thing—step by step and day by day!

Chapter 5

Risk

Get Out of Your Safe Zone

Jean Hanson and her husband, Steve, were celebrating their anniversary at a beautiful beach resort in St. Lucia. One morning they decided to walk the resort's Wellness Trail—a one-mile path with stations for exercises like pull-ups, a balance beam, and even an elevated rope bridge. At each station they did the activity. Then they came to the rope bridge. Steve crossed it easily, but Jean hesitated.

"All I could see were big gaping holes on the sides, large enough to fit my entire leg through with one slip of the foot," she wrote. Fear overcame her, and she backed off and walked away, frustrated and disappointed in herself.

The next day she and Steve took a trip on a twenty-four-foot sailboat. It was Jean's first time sailing and she was thrilled and exhilarated, even when the boat was in choppy waters. Experienced sailors were in charge, but Jean knew this adventure was far more dangerous than the rope bridge she'd backed away from.

The following morning, Jean and Steve took the Wellness Trail again. "This time I didn't say anything, just walked up the ladder and went for it. I didn't stop to look at it and wonder how I was going to accomplish this feat. I just paused for a second on the platform, grabbed the rope and started putting one foot in front of the other. . . . Before I knew it, I was across feeling victorious!"

The experience helped Jean realize something about herself. "Looking back, I realized this wasn't the first time I'd done this. There have been several times throughout my life that instead of wallowing in worry or fearing what might happen, I simply paused for a moment, made a decision and immediately took action. In those moments, I realized I'm much stronger than I give myself credit for."[1]

Most of us think of risk as a negative situation we should avoid. But risk is part of life, and it's a big part of faith. Not every risk is worth taking, but if you're too overwhelmed by fear to correctly assess a situation, you'll miss many opportunities for growth, increased strength, deeper faith, and success.

Have you been playing it safe? Too safe? If forward is the direction you choose, be prepared to take some faith-based risks. Being a follower of Christ in today's world is not safe. And it isn't intended to be.

In his book *Seizing Your Divine Moment*, Erwin McManus wrote, "I want to reiterate the fact that the center of God's will is not a safe place, but the most dangerous place in the world. God fears nothing and no one. God moves with intentionality and power. To live outside God's will puts us in danger, but to live in His will makes us dangerous."[2]

Think of the people in Scripture who took great risks. Moses wasn't playing it safe when he returned to Egypt to confront Pharaoh (Ex. 5:1). Gideon wasn't playing it safe when he dismissed most of his army (Judg. 7:7). David wasn't playing it safe when he strode up to Goliath (1 Sam. 17:32). Shadrach, Meshach, and Abednego weren't playing it safe when they refused to bow down to the image Nebuchadnezzar had erected in the Babylonian plains (Dan. 3:16–18). Esther wasn't playing it safe when she put her life on the line to save her people, telling Mordecai, "If I perish, I perish" (Est. 4:16). Peter wasn't playing it safe when he stepped out of the fishing boat to walk across the water to Jesus (Matt. 14:29). Paul wasn't playing it safe when he preached to Governor Felix about "righteousness, self-control, and the judgment to come" (Acts 24:25). The apostle John wasn't playing it safe in his old age when he sent a book from Patmos filled with images of dragons, beasts, and coming days of wrath and judgment.

You can't play it safe either. Not if you want to seize tomorrow and accomplish the dreams God places in your heart. As we saw in the previous chapter, you'll need to focus if you want to move forward toward those dreams. In this chapter, we'll see why taking risks is also necessary.

Mr. Risk-Taker

In the work God has given me through the years, I've had to make a lot of difficult decisions. Left to myself, I might have erred too often on the side of safety and security. But there's a man in the Bible who inspires me to keep stepping out and taking risks with wholehearted confidence in the Lord. I'm convinced you'll be able to go forward—unafraid to take risks—if you can embody his spirit.

That man is Caleb. Do you know him? Many people don't know a great deal about Caleb, because he only occupies thirty verses in the Bible. But what verses they are! What a man of faith! In this chapter, I want to show you how this Old Testament hero left a legacy of courage for you—a powerful example of risk-taking, future-grabbing grace.

In the book of Numbers, Moses sent twelve men—Joshua, Caleb, and ten others—as an advance party to reconnoiter the promised land. These men left the safety of their encampment, forded the Jordan River, and slipped into Canaan. Their mission: to make notes of the land, observe the enemy, study the fortifications, estimate the population, and bring back enough intelligence to aid Moses in planning the coming invasion of the land God had promised the Israelites.

The Bible tells the story this way: "So they went up and explored the land from the wilderness of Zin. . . . Going north, they passed through the Negev and arrived at Hebron, where Ahiman, Sheshai, and Talmai—all descendants of Anak—lived" (Num. 13:21–22 NLT).

The city of Hebron had been the ancestral home of Abraham, Isaac, and Jacob, but now it was inhabited by an evil tribe of huge warriors known as the descendants of Anak. The sight of these warriors terrified some of the spies.

The scouts quickly harvested some pomegranates and figs from the orchards of Canaan, and two of them lugged back an enormous cluster of grapes, carrying it on a pole between them. Imagine the excitement when the spies returned to Kadesh Barnea! Their mission had taken forty days, during which no one knew if they had survived or perished. Day after day, sentries at Israel's parameters watched for them. Now they were back—all of them safe and sound.

But they were not united.

How to Live Life in the Safe Zone

In professional football, NFL coaches study the smallest statistic to find every possible advantage. But according to author John Tierney and research psychologist Roy F. Baumeister, many coaches make the same simple mistake week after week. It happens on fourth-down-and-short situations, when their team only needs a yard or two to keep possession of the ball. Nine times out of ten, instead of the riskier decision to try to win by going for another score, the coach settles for trying not to lose and sends in the kicker to punt the ball to the other team.

Statistics show that trying for the goal and the win is actually the better strategy. So why do coaches punt on fourth down? Tierney and

Baumeister concluded there's another factor involved. They call it "the power of bad."

Simply put, our brains are wired to give more importance to negative events than positive ones. So "bad" events influence our decision-making more than positive ones. That means no matter how much we want to succeed, avoiding "bad" events can easily become our primary goal.

Back to the coach. He knows if he chooses the risky play and fails, and the other team goes on to score, the fans and press will be unforgiving. Sportscasters will denounce him as reckless and use phrases like *loss of momentum* and the *turning point* in the game. If his team loses by a narrow margin, that failed fourth-down attempt will be blamed for the loss and replayed endlessly afterward.

That image of potential failure is hard to overcome. So the coach plays it safe. The fear of failure has lost many a game.[3]

Have you ever heard these names: Shammua, Shaphat, Igal, Palti, Gaddiel, Gaddi, Ammiel, Sethur, Nahbi, and Geuel? No? These are the names of the ten spies who risked their lives on an espionage mission only to lose heart, doubt God's power, and miss God's will (Num. 13:4–15). They came back so discouraged they disheartened the people of Israel.

Those men made three terrible mistakes. They fell into three traps you and I must avoid at all costs.

Maximize the Opposition

God wants you to go forward. He has adventures, challenges, victories, and meaningful tasks for you. As you look at the bridge to your future, are you looking at the ropes or at the holes? Jean Hanson wrote, "If you're one of those people that are afraid to take calculated risks, worry about every little thing, and have a hard time making decisions in your life, it's time to take a break and do a little work on yourself. . . . I learned a long time ago that being timid and conservative will get you nowhere."[4]

In Numbers 13, the ten spies magnified every threat. They looked at the "bridge" God had designed for the future, and all they saw were the holes. The Bible says,

> But the men who had gone up with him said, "We are not able to go up against the people, for they are stronger than we." And they gave the children of Israel a bad report of the land which they had spied out, saying, "The land through which we have gone as spies is a land that devours its inhabitants, and all the people whom we saw in it are men of great stature. There we saw the giants (the descendants of Anak came from the giants); and we were like grasshoppers in our own sight, and so we were in their sight." (Num. 13:31–33)

Notice all the *holes* the ten unbelieving spies fixated on:

- We are not able to go up against these people.
- They are stronger than we are.
- The land devours its inhabitants.
- The men are of great stature.
- The men are giants.
- They are from Anak, the land of giants.
- We are like grasshoppers in our eyes.
- We are like grasshoppers in their eyes.

If you propose to move forward in life, especially if you aspire to leadership, you'll have to learn what it means to take risks—to live by faith. Scripture says, "For God has not given us a spirit of fear and timidity, but of power, love, and self-discipline" (2 Tim. 1:7 NLT). Even history's most celebrated leaders had to learn this lesson.

At the beginning of the Civil War, no military career looked brighter than General George B. McClellan's, whom some called the "Napoleon of the American Republic." Lincoln made him commander of the Army of the Potomac, and later promoted him to be the first general-in-chief of the Union Army.

McClellan cut a stunning figure on horseback; he looked like he'd been selected by central casting for the role. But he also regularly overestimated the size of the enemy, magnifying the threat. The more daunting the enemy grew in his mind, the less confidence he showed in the field. He saw the holes instead of the ropes.

Although he constantly organized and prepared, he rarely got around to fighting. When he did, his objective seemed to be avoiding a loss, not winning the battle. Lincoln finally wrote McClellan, saying, "If you don't want to use the army, I should like to borrow it for a while."[5]

Hmm . . . remind you of the ten spies?

More importantly, now is a good time to ask yourself if it reminds you of—well, you? Whenever we compare ourselves to the opposition, instead of comparing the opposition to God, we can get into a state of fear. If that's a pattern in your life, the first step forward is recognizing it.

When Jesus left Galilee to travel to Jerusalem near the end of His life, "His face was set for the journey to Jerusalem" (Luke 9:53). Jesus knew the cross awaited, yet there was no looking back for our Lord, no comparing, and no fear. His way forward was clear and He faced it head on.

You must do the same. Recognize the risk and properly evaluate the opposition. Then, when you have an inkling of God's will for your life, set your face toward it and go forward.

Minimize the Opportunities

While the ten spies maximized the opposition, they also minimized the glorious opportunities that lay ahead of them. They only had a dim perception of what God had in store for them; they believed in their hearts that God was setting them up for destruction, and their unbelief was contagious.

You can read it for yourself in Numbers 14: "So all the congregation lifted up their voices and cried, and the people wept that night. And all the children of Israel complained against Moses and Aaron, and the whole congregation said to them, 'If only we had died in the land of Egypt! Or if only we had died in this wilderness! Why has the LORD brought us to this land to fall by the sword, that our wives and children should become victims? Would it not be better for us to return to Egypt?'" (vv. 1–3).

Their perception of God would be laughable if it weren't so tragic. After all the Lord had done for them! He delivered them from slavery! Parted the wide waters of the Red Sea! Accompanied them with cloud and fire! Gave them His Law! Provided food and drink in the wilderness! Promised to make them a great nation in a land flowing with milk and honey!

How could they so quickly forget?

More importantly, how can we? When we forget all the blessings God has provided for us in the past, we're apt to minimize His ability to guide us in the future. We may even dread the future and where we think God is leading us. If so, we're exactly where the devil wants us: in a place of avoiding risks and playing it safe. Oh, we of little faith.

What I'm telling you is this: don't minimize the opportunities God has for you in the future. Don't put all your efforts into avoiding loss or turn your face away from the future He has planned for you. Instead, go forward with confidence and courage to do the task He has set for you.

Jeopardize the Objective

In their unbelief, the Israelites discarded the precious, powerful future God intended for them. Their act of defiant unbelief incurred a terrible penalty.

The punishment for bringing an evil report to the people of God was meted out in two severe sentences. First, the ten men who gave the evil report were killed immediately by a plague: "Now the men whom Moses sent to spy out the land, who returned and made all the congregation complain against him by bringing a bad report of the land, those very men who brought the evil report about the land, died by the plague before the LORD. But Joshua the son of Nun and Caleb the son of Jephunneh remained alive, of the men who went to spy out the land" (Num. 14:36–38).

Second, the children of Israel who listened to the ten spies and refused to go forward were also penalized. The Lord said, "You will all drop dead in this wilderness! Because you complained against me, every one of you who is twenty years or older and was included in the registration will die. You will not enter and occupy the land I swore to give you. The only exceptions will be Caleb . . . and Joshua" (Num. 14:29–30 NLT).

How very sad! The blessing God wanted to pour out upon His people was forfeited by their unwillingness to risk obedience to His command.

What is your Canaan? What does God want you to tackle, to possess, to accomplish for Him? Unbelief forfeits your opportunities and jeopardizes your objective.

So let's keep seizing the moments God provides for us with child-like wonder.

How to Risk Life in the Faith Zone

And that brings us back to courageous Caleb. He and Joshua represented the minority opinion among the spies. Caleb had pleaded with the people, "Let us go up at once and take possession, for we are well able to overcome it" (Num. 13:30). Imagine Caleb's frustration when the whole nation shouted down his words!

But God heard. As the decades passed, one by one the older Israelites passed away, and their bodies dotted the desert. Even the aged Moses ascended Mount Pisgah and died. Joshua and Caleb were the sole survivors of their generation, but when the day came to lead Israel into the promised land they were as young in spirit as forty years before. Joshua succeeded Moses and led the Israelites across the Jordan River and into the land of Canaan. As we read through the book of Joshua, we find conquest after conquest, and allotment after allotment.

Then we open the Bible to Joshua 14, and who should we meet again but Caleb. He made a trip to see his old friend and fellow spy, Joshua, and said:

> You know what the LORD said to Moses the man of God at Kadesh Barnea about you and me. I was forty years old when Moses the servant of the LORD sent me from Kadesh Barnea to explore the land. And I brought him back a report according to my convictions, but my fellow Israelites who went up with me made the hearts of the people melt in fear. I, however, followed the LORD my God wholeheartedly. So on that day Moses swore to me, "The land on which your feet have walked will be your inheritance and that of your children forever, because you have followed the LORD my God wholeheartedly." (Josh. 14:6–9 NIV)

With the passing of the years, Caleb's faith had grown. His mind was sharp, his spirit strong, and his enthusiasm like a child's. The promise of God was still the obsession of his heart. I believe there are four reasons for this, and they help us understand what is involved in living a life of risk.

Risk-Takers Stay Exuberant About Their Lives

The first reason has to do with Caleb's exuberance. He told Joshua, "Now then, just as the LORD promised, he has kept me alive for forty-five years. . . . So here I am today, eighty-five years old! I am still as strong today as the day Moses sent me out; I'm just as vigorous to go out to battle now as I was then" (Josh. 14:10–11 NIV).

Can you feel the energy that fueled Caleb's life? He was as courageous at eighty-five as at forty. When you have that exuberance, age and abilities become background to achievement.

After watching the 1996 Olympics, actress Geena Davis became intrigued with the sport of archery. Although she'd played athletes in films, she wasn't what you'd call athletic in her personal life. But at age forty-one, something about archery gripped her imagination.

"I found a coach and became utterly obsessed," she says. Davis began practicing five or six hours a day, five or six days a week. Two and a half years later, she competed in the semifinals for a spot on the US Olympic archery team in hopes of going to the 2000 Olympics in Sydney, Australia. She placed twenty-fourth out of three hundred, narrowly missing a spot on the team.

"If you risk nothing, then you risk everything," Davis has said.[6]

Now that's exuberance!

Psychologist Kay Redfield Jamison wrote, "Exuberance carries us places we would not otherwise go—across the savannah, to the moon, into the imagination. . . . By its pleasures, exuberance lures us from our common places and quieter moods; and—after the victory, the harvest, the discovery of a new idea or an unfamiliar place—it gives ascendant reason to venture forth all over again."[7]

That's a description of Caleb, and I hope it's a description of you. It's hard to go forward without the kind of joyful zest for life Caleb had. That same joyful eagerness is possible for you too.

"For me?" you say.

Yes, it is! You can't lose the wonder of the worshipful, promise-filled life Christ died to give you. You can ask God for joy, and you can choose to be exuberant in life based on His promises. It's not a matter of conjuring up emotions, it's a matter of saying, "Lord, with Your help, I'm going to be like Joshua and Caleb, not like the other ten."

Risk-Takers Stay Excited About Their Futures

Following as naturally as thunder behind lightning, when you're exuberant about your life you're excited about your future. Exhibit

A: Caleb. He didn't visit with his old friend just to reminisce about the past. He had the future in mind. Something specific had arisen in his heart. Let's eavesdrop on their conversation.

Caleb told Joshua, "Now give me this hill country that the LORD promised me that day. You yourself heard then that the Anakites were there and their cities were large and fortified, but, the LORD helping me, I will drive them out just as he said" (Josh. 14:12 NIV).

When I read that I feel like shouting, "Yes!" At age eighty-five, Caleb was ready to claim the hill country, tame the land, and provide a lasting inheritance for his children.

There's something here I don't want you to miss. Earlier in the chapter, I mentioned that the city of Hebron had been the ancestral home of Abraham, Isaac, and Jacob, but now it was inhabited by an evil tribe of huge warriors known as the descendants of Anak. The sight of these warriors had terrified the ten unfaithful spies, who felt like grasshoppers compared to the enemy. This portion of territory was still untaken by Israel, unpossessed, unclaimed. The giants had scared everyone away.

Everyone except old Caleb, who said, in effect, "I want that hill country as my inheritance, and I'm ready to take care of those daunting supervillains. Let me at them!"

No matter your age or circumstances, no matter what hill you need to take, that kind of enthusiasm will carry you forward.

Jessica Long was orphaned in Siberia as an infant. Born with fibular hemimelia, she didn't have fibulas, ankles, heels, or most of the bones in her feet. But after much prayer, a Christian couple from Baltimore, Maryland, Steve and Beth Long, adopted her when she was thirteen months old. A few months later, Jessica's legs were amputated below the knees.

Growing up, she couldn't do everything other children did, but she learned to swim without prosthetics in her grandparents' pool. At age ten, Jessica joined a swim team. At twelve, she won three gold medals in the 2004 Paralympic Games in Athens. Since then she's competed in three more Paralympic Games, and her medal count is up to thirteen gold, six silver, and four bronze. She's one of America's most decorated Olympians.

"I was raised the right way," Jessica said, "but I still had to come to Christ on my own. Eventually I decided I wanted to give Jesus my whole heart. It was the best decision I've ever made."

And she has some advice for us: "Believe you are capable of incredible things and that God has a plan for every individual. I want you to embrace who God made you to be. . . . I now look at my legs and think of all the people I've been able to touch because God made me this way. Embrace who you are! Shine bright and never ever give up on your dreams."[8]

Jessica looks back with gratitude, but her focus is on the future: "I'm so excited for what's next," she told a reporter.[9]

Someone said, "If you can get excited about the future, the past won't matter." Even when the world is coming apart at the seams; when global panics and pandemics are the order of the day; when our economy is uncertain and our faith is under assault; even then—especially then—you need to look ahead to the next step God has for you.

Caleb didn't use his gray hair to beg off the heavy lifting. He asked for a worthy challenge because he had the wisdom to know that with a powerful quest comes powerful reward. Knock down a giant and you become a giant yourself. He still had a vision for the future, and because of that he accomplished the greatest victory of his life at age eighty-five.

Risk-Takers Stay Enthusiastic About Their Assignment

As you can see, Caleb was enthusiastic about his assignment. Joshua and the Israelites had not yet succeeded in driving the evil occupants out of large sections of the promised land. The business was unfinished. But Joshua 15:14 says, "Caleb drove out the three sons of Anak from there: Sheshai, Ahiman, and Talmai, the children of

Anak." Caleb did exactly what he was told, and he did it immediately. He is one of those success stories whose secret is not so secret. He just did it in the strength of the Lord! That's enthusiasm!

Today our ministries at Turning Point cover the globe because of the capabilities of worldwide broadcasting. Much of the technological credit goes to Sir Edward Appleton, whose scientific discoveries won him a Nobel Prize in 1947. When asked about the secret of his lasting accomplishments, he said, "It was enthusiasm. I rate enthusiasm even above professional skill."[10]

Enthusiasm is a word that is made up of the Greek words for *in* and *God—En-theos-ism*. It was coined to describe the zeal of the early Christians. When we have the God of all energy within us, there's a surge of power that's like an atomic reaction in our hearts. The apostle Paul said, "I strenuously contend with all the energy Christ so power-fully works in me" (Col. 1:29 NIV).

Several years ago, a Florida newspaper profiled seventy-one-year-old designer Lileth Hogarth. She grew up watching her mother sew clothes for her family in Jamaica, and Lileth has kept people in stitches ever since—literally. "You're never dead until you're dead," Lileth said. "And you should keep your dream alive as long as you are alive."[11]

Risk-Takers Stay Energized About Their God

And that brings us to the consummation of our story. Only the energy of our God within us can keep us barreling forward into the remainder of God's will for our lives. As I said, the story of Caleb's life is told in thirty verses in the Bible. But six times in those verses (with my emphases added) we're given the secret to his risk-filled, risk-taking life:

- "But My servant Caleb . . . has a different spirit in him and has *followed Me fully*" (Num. 14:24).
- "They have not wholly followed Me, except Caleb the son of

Jephunneh, the Kenizzite, and Joshua the son of Nun, for they have *wholly followed* the LORD" (Num. 32:11–12).

- "Caleb the son of Jephunneh; he shall see it, and to him and his children I am giving the land on which he walked, because he *wholly followed* the LORD" (Deut. 1:36).
- "I *wholly followed* the LORD my God. So Moses swore on that day, saying, 'Surely the land where your foot has trodden shall be your inheritance and your children's forever, because you have *wholly followed* the LORD my God'" (Josh. 14:8–9).
- "Hebron therefore became the inheritance of Caleb the son of Jephunneh the Kenizzite to this day, because he *wholly followed* the LORD God of Israel" (Josh. 14:14).

Caleb wholly followed . . . wholly followed . . . wholly followed . . . wholly followed! By the time he was eighty-five, most of his generation had given up hope and died. But Caleb still had a bright fire burning. He still wanted to risk his life on the greatest possible task God could give him.

As I reflect on what it means to incorporate risk into our walk with God, I want to tell you a story about the church I serve: Shadow Mountain Community Church in El Cajon, California. By 1990, I'd been the pastor there for about ten years. After almost eight years of struggling, we were finally ready to move into our new worship center. We knew we'd experience dramatic growth and we tried to prepare for it. Finances were on our minds, of course. But we were concerned that our giving to worldwide evangelization not suffer. In fact, we wanted to increase it. But how?

At that time, many people wrote two checks each pay period to our church—one for our church budget and the other to our missionary budget. But I foresaw a day when people could give to the church knowing that a portion of every gift would automatically go to worldwide evangelism.

During a business meeting, someone suggested we allocate five percent of our general budget to missions. Someone else suggested we give ten percent. After all, we asked people to tithe (or give ten percent) of their income to the Lord. Why should not a church tithe of its income to missions?

That seemed like a big risk. With our new building payments and our growing ministry, we were struggling to meet our financial obligations. How would we ever survive if we took ten percent of our already not-enough budget and gave it away?

That's when I heard myself get up and say, "What do you think God would do for us if we gave twenty percent of our budget to missions going forward?" This was a long time ago, but I still remember how quiet it got in that room—and how quiet it stayed.

Then a man by the name of Ralph Radford spoke up. He was a Caleb. He encouraged us to take up that challenge. He predicted God would bless us if we did. Someone else reminded us that missions is the closest thing to the heart of God in the Bible. God had sent His own Son into this world as the first missionary. We made that decision—the kind of risk I've been talking about—and have carried it out without interruption for thirty years.

Today Shadow Mountain currently supports 198 missionary families with ministries in 41 countries and in over 50 different languages. We help to underwrite three pregnancy care centers, the downtown rescue mission, the servicemen's center, and our Spanish-speaking, Arabic-speaking, and Iranian congregations. Our missions budget this year will exceed four million dollars, and over the years since we took that risk our church has given over $51 million to help evangelize the world.

None of that is said to boast. It's said in thanksgiving but also as a lesson for all of us. We made a decision to take a risk and win, and not just to try and avoid losing. God honored that decision in a magnificent way.

What risk is God leading you to take as you go forward? His will for you is not earthly comfort but divine courage. Courage in the face of opposition. Courage in the face of cultural change. Courage when confronted with the unknown. Courage in the midst of a pandemic. God will never choose safety for us if it will cost significance. God created us to count, not to be counted.

This is your time to move forward, out of the safe zone and into the faith zone.

Chapter 6

Pursue

Chase Your Dream

Paddy Kelly grew up surrounded by music. The tenth child in an American family living in Ireland, he joined his older siblings' band, the Kelly Family, at a young age. When he was fifteen, he wrote a song that propelled the family to stardom, and the group became a global sensation. With money and fame came great opportunities, such as singing in stadiums to 250,000 screaming fans.

In time, Paddy moved into a seventeenth-century castle. He traveled by private plane and helicopter. His family was near him in his pursuits, and he was never far from their love. Yet something strange happened. Paddy felt empty, lost. The higher he rose the lower he felt. He asked himself a haunting question: "If all this doesn't make me happy, then what is the sense of life. Why do I exist?"

He eventually retired to a monastery in France seeking answers.[1]

Joseph Schooling is one of the best swimmers in the world. His youthful face and friendly grin make him a crowd favorite—especially after he won Singapore's first-ever Olympic gold medal in 2016. He's one of a small group of people who breathe the rarefied air of being the best in the world.

But how does it feel to be a gold medalist? According to Schooling, there's a "feeling of emptiness." Schooling concedes he didn't know how to respond to fame and pressure. "I should have taken more time away from the pool," he said. "I had to change my mindset as I was no longer chasing, I was being chased. . . . I needed to find my 'why' for what I was doing."[2]

Like Paddy Kelly and Joseph Schooling, millions of people are searching for the *why* of their existence. Maybe that includes you.

In chapter one I wrote about your dreams and how to build a vision for your future. Your vision answers the "What?" questions: *What could my life look like in the future? What do I see myself doing?*

Now I encourage you to pursue your purpose. Your purpose is about *meaning* and *motivation*. It's the reason behind your actions and decisions. It answers that nagging "Why?" question. *Why am I pursuing this dream?* Paddy Kelly knew the *what* of his life—singing. Joseph knew the *what* of his life—swimming. But they couldn't figure out the *why*. Was it for applause? Money? Achievement? Self-fulfillment? National pride?

Your vision keeps your hopes alive; it's your dream of a better tomorrow. Your purpose gives you strength to move forward even when times are tough. Purpose stabilizes your life. With a clear purpose, you persevere because you know there's a reason, a cause.

Do you ever end the day, or the year, asking yourself, "What was all that for? What did I really accomplish? What difference did I truly make?" When you find your purpose, you stop chasing things that will never satisfy you. Instead, you find the joy of pursuing the next steps God has for you.

What if you could close out the day, the month, and the year knowing you're fulfilling your true purpose and calling in life? Imagine being certain beyond doubt that your efforts weren't wasted because they were God-conceived, God-directed, and God-honoring.

What Paddy Kelly and Joseph Schooling longed for, Jesus possessed. He knew He was placed on earth for a reason, and He pursued His God-ordained purpose at every step. In Mark 1:38, He told His disciples, "Let us go into the next towns, that I may preach there also, because for this purpose I have come forth."

In John 12:27, He prayed, "Now My soul is troubled, and what shall I say? 'Father, save Me from this hour'? But for this purpose I came to this hour."

The apostle John said, "For this purpose the Son of God was manifested, that He might destroy the works of the devil" (1 John 3:8).

Jesus knew His purpose in life, and He was compelled to fulfill it. You also can have this sense of certainty to move you toward your goal. You can do what Jesus did, and you can live the rest of your life with no regrets.

How do you discover your "why"? Your journey begins by committing your life to God.

Present Yourself Totally to God

Manny Pacquiao is one of the greatest professional boxers of all time. He is the only eight-division world champion in the history of boxing. Yet along with his fame came gambling, sex, money, and parties. But his heart was as vacant as a boxing arena after all the people left and the lights were turned off. "I felt empty," he said. "I had money. I could do whatever I wanted, but I was empty in my heart."

One night while walking in a forest, the Filipino boxer was convicted about his lifestyle. He knelt down and cried out to God, asking for forgiveness and help. He later said he felt like a light was shining on him as bright as the sun, but he couldn't raise his head. He was on the ground crying out to the Lord. He felt he was melting.

That night, Christ came into Manny Pacquiao's life. "The Lord changed my heart," he says.[3]

Pacquiao's life took on new meaning. He became involved in public service and today serves in the Philippine national senate. During the coronavirus pandemic, he donated hundreds of thousands of masks to those in need, along with five buses to transport healthcare workers around Manila. He felt such an immense burden for the poor that he determined to care for them even if he died in the effort. He told his constituents, "We should . . . continue praying and believing in the Lord. Let's all draw strength and hope from Him."[4]

You can't find your purpose in life by focusing on yourself and leaving God out of the picture. Life isn't about using God for your purposes. It's about God using you for His purposes. It's about the Lord Jesus showing you how you fit into His plan. And you do fit in! He has a lifetime of purpose stored up for you.

Perhaps you're thinking, "I'm not sure I want to be in God's plan. What if I don't like it?"

Oh, you will! It's what you were made for. If you don't embrace God's plan, you'll miss the purpose for which He created you. The Bible is clear about that. Jesus said, "I am the light of the world. He who follows Me shall not walk in darkness, but have the light of life" (John 8:12). When you follow God's plan for your life, you will be walking in the divine wattage of God's light. There's no other source of ultimate purpose. All other pursuits lead to darkness and futility.

Are you still afraid to present yourself totally to God? Do you still think He'll mess up your life by telling you to do something you don't want to do—or to go somewhere you don't want to go?

I can tell you by my own testimony that everything I ever dreamed of doing in my life I found in God's purpose for me. I cannot imagine doing anything else than what I've done as He has led me. So many of my dreams have come true, plus quite a few dreams I didn't even know I had.

The first step toward pursuing your God-given purpose is to present yourself totally to God. He loves you. He wants the best for you. You can trust Him!

Understand Your Uniqueness

The second step in discovering the "Why?" of your life is coming to grips with the unique *you.*

Rick Allen was a world-famous drummer with Def Leppard, one of the most successful rock groups of the last generation. He joined the group when he was only fifteen, and the band sold over one hundred million albums. But in 1984, at the height of his young career, Allen was trying to pass an aggressive driver on a narrow road in England, and he had a horrific wreck. His arm was severed in the crash. Doctors tried to reattach it, but it became infected and had to be amputated.

Now Allen was a one-armed drummer, but he didn't give up. He devised ways to compensate for his loss and became even better and even more appreciated by his fans. Then Allen took up painting, and his art became valued by collectors. Allen says he creates art the way he drums—with one arm and an open heart. "I don't want to compare myself to others," he says. "I want to celebrate my uniqueness."[5]

Every single person on this planet can celebrate their uniqueness because God didn't create any two people—not even identical twins—who are exactly alike. We all have different bodies, different faces, different fingerprints, different backgrounds, different gifts and talents.

There is no one like you!

Only you have the unique plan God has designed for *you.* Ephesians 2:10 says, "For we are God's handiwork, created in Christ Jesus to do good works, which God prepared in advance for us to do" (NIV). The New Living Translation says, "For we are God's masterpiece. He has created us anew in Christ Jesus, so we can do the good things he planned for us long ago."

Stop and read that again. You are God's masterpiece. Before you were born, He designed a set of tasks for you. He created you for your life's purpose, and at the same time He was creating your work for you.

Not for anyone else. Just for you.

For that reason, beware of comparing yourself with others. There's almost always someone who seems more gifted or more successful than you, and if you're not careful you can slip into imitating that person without even realizing it. But you are not an imitation. You are the original, the only you God ever made.

As a young preacher, I studied my homiletics professor, Haddon Robinson, who was a master in the pulpit. I also took classes from Howard Hendricks, who was the best communicator I'd ever heard. Sure enough, without realizing it, when I prepared and preached my early sermons I sounded a lot like Haddon or Howard. I didn't realize I was imitating them, but my wife, Donna, noticed it. We had a little conversation, and I realized I could only be David Jeremiah. I had to learn to be myself—to be the person God created me to be.

E. E. Cummings said, "To be nobody-but-yourself—in a world which is doing its best, night and day, to make you everybody else—means to fight the hardest battle which any human being can fight; and never stop fighting."[6]

If you look at somebody else for the pattern of who you should be, you're missing something. God made you special, and then He threw away the plans. Thank Him for your strengths and weaknesses, your blessings and burdens, your gifts and talents, your experience and adventures. And offer them all to Him for His use and for His glory.

Once you understand the uniqueness of you, you'll be well on your way to pursuing the purpose God created just for you.

Realize Your Responsibility

The next step is to realize that your uniqueness implies action. The Bible says, "As each one has received a gift, minister it to one another, as good stewards of the manifold grace of God" (1 Pet. 4:10). In other words, God has given you a gift, and with that gift comes a responsibility to use it to bless others.

Many people resent having responsibilities placed on them. But don't let the devil deceive you. Your responsibilities—the ones that come from God—are blessings, for they reassure you of your usefulness. As someone said, *responsibility* is your response to God's ability.

Michael Lee, a graduate of Azusa Pacific University, served the Lord in every way he could during his college years, then he got a job at the Duncan Toys Company. But how could he fulfill his God-given responsibility for divine service at a toy company? Well, Michael became a professional yo-yoer, and over time he shared the gospel with over 1.7 million children in all fifty states, and even performed three times at the White House. And then after a near-fatal skiing accident, Michael signed up for grueling Spartan Races, where he finds new opportunities to share his story and inspire others to look to Christ and persevere.[7]

No one else has a story or a set of responsibilities exactly like those except him.

Chris Baker has a unique set of responsibilities too. He's a Chicago-area tattoo artist who came to Jesus Christ as an adult. He began leading a Young Life group at his church and often told his teens to pray to know the next thing God wanted them to do. He told them the Lord made each of them for a purpose.[8]

One day Chris realized he needed to take his own advice, so he began praying for God to show him the next step—what *he* alone could do. It dawned on him that many former gang members were ashamed and hindered by their tattoos, so he began a ministry of covering those evil markings with works of art. His ministry is called INK 180, and through it he's helping many young men escape their pasts, disconnect from gangs, and start new lives. Some have also started new lives in Christ.

The Department of Homeland Security's gang division became intrigued by Chris's work. One day while visiting their headquarters, Chris discovered another need. From the unit that investigates human trafficking crimes, Chris was stunned to learn that hundreds of young women, including many domestic violence victims and runaways, are held captive by organized crime members and gangs. Often they're tattooed by their captors so they can be identified and returned if they try to escape. Sometimes the tattoos are literally bar codes, and sometimes the victims are branded or scarred like animals. Chris became heartbroken during the briefing. He didn't know such brutality existed, and he longed to help these young women.

Chris and his INK 180 ministry began meeting with victims of abuse, covering their vile markings with beautiful artwork of flowers and other images, and giving them an opportunity to escape their pasts and find freedom in Christ.[9]

No one else has a story or a set of responsibilities exactly like these except Chris. Trust me, you don't want David Jeremiah coming at you with a tattoo needle!

You see, the church is a big circle made up of all God's children, and every one of us has a responsibility. The Bible says, "A spiritual gift is given to each of us so we can help each other" (1 Cor. 12:7 NLT).

Jesus said, "As long as it is day, we must do the works of him who sent me. Night is coming, when no one can work" (John 9:4 NIV). Let yourself develop a sense of responsibility for reaching others and serving the world, and make that decision before "night" falls on your life—before it's too late.

Pursue God's Plan for Your Life

If you've presented yourself totally to God, grasped the wonderful fact of your uniqueness, and realized you have a responsibility to serve the Lord and others, then you're ready to pursue God's plan for your life. Now your task is to chase that plan. You have to run in the direction your purpose leads you.

When I sensed in my heart God was calling me to preach the gospel, I immediately made an appointment with Dr. Robert Gromacki, a teacher in the Bible department of the college I attended. He was a great professor, young and vibrant. He'd graduated from Dallas Theological Seminary, and he helped me make connections there that I pursued so that I would have the training necessary to obey God's call.

When you begin to sense God leading you in a certain direction, don't be apathetic or passive about it. Be active. Ask questions. Make visits. Garner advice. Read. Study. Look for the next steps and take them. Don't wait for God to interrupt your television program with a special bulletin telling you what to do.

David Groves was the chief of police in Hartford, Wisconsin, capping off a career in law enforcement. As he approached retirement he thought, *But now what?* His entire life had been devoted to public safety. Because of the dangerous and rigorous nature of the job, many police officers retire earlier than other professionals, and David felt he still had many productive years ahead of him. What should he do?

He and his wife prayed, knowing God had blessed them both throughout their careers. They pondered Proverbs 16:9 and sought opportunities while trusting God to lead them. David began to wonder if his experiences might be helpful on a church staff. As chief of police, he'd learned the principles of good management, strategic planning, participatory leadership, wisdom, empathy, and vision to accomplish a mission. He'd learned to manage a budget and get along with competing factions.

David began researching the possibility of becoming an executive pastor in a church. He studied job descriptions to learn more. The more he pursued God's plan for him, the more he saw opportunities. Today, the former police chief is now the executive pastor of a church in Wisconsin—and you'd better not speed past his sanctuary!

"If you're not dead, you're not done when it comes to serving the Lord," David said. "As far as God's nudge goes, it would be hard to share all the times we have seen his hand in this process, over and [over]. Suffice to say, every door has opened at just the right time, every challenge has quickly been overcome, and both my wife and I have had real peace about this decision since the beginning."

"In my . . . former line of work, we would call these things 'clues,'" he added.[10]

That's a great way of looking at it. In a sense, God gives us clues about His purpose and plans for our lives. As you consider your next steps forward, remember—if you're not dead, you're not done. Keep pursuing God's good, acceptable, and perfect plan for your life. Look for indications. Notice circumstances. Follow leads. Take initiative.

Look around you right now. Do you see any clues to follow?

Obey Orders from God's Word

That brings us to the next critical element of pursuing God's purpose for your life. You have to obey orders from His Word. His will for your life never deviates from the Word He has given you in Scripture. You'll need instructions for the journey, and God's instruction manual is your Bible.

Joshua 1:8 says, "This Book of the Law shall not depart from your mouth, but you shall meditate in it day and night, that you may observe to do according to all that is written in it. For then you will make your way prosperous, and then you will have good success."

Notice the phrase *observe to do*. It's easy to pass over these words as unimportant, but they present one of the great concepts of the Old Testament. We're not to read the Bible just for curiosity or intellectual reasons alone. We're to study it to discover God's will for our lives. We read it to heed it!

David described this principle in his first psalm: "His delight is in the law of the LORD, and in His law he meditates day and night. He shall be like a tree planted by the rivers of water, that brings forth its fruit in its season, whose leaf also shall not wither; and whatever he does shall prosper" (Ps. 1:2–3).

Popular author Eddie Jones has a park bench beneath a willow tree at his house where, in his words, he goes to get his orders every day. Even in the winter when the garden feels "more like a Popsicle than paradise," he opens his Bible and asks God for a ray of light on his day and a beam of divine guidance for his steps. He prays, "May your kingdom come, may your will be done, on earth and in my life, in the same way your will is done in heaven. Lead me to where you would have me to serve you today."

Then Eddie opens his Bible. "I study each verse of Scripture, searching for promises, commands, warnings, praise, prayers, and words of comfort. When I sense His voice whispering, 'Pay attention, this is important,' I highlight the verse and write it in my journal. Then I ponder its meaning for me that day."[11]

Now, you don't have to sit on a cold bench, but you do need to find your own process. As you pursue God's purpose for your life there will be times when you feel lost, when you don't know what to do next. You'll be confused—perhaps even disoriented. It's in those times especially that you'll learn to love the Word of God. That's why it's important to have a daily habit of Bible reading and meditation.

It's not that you'll find a Bible verse that says, "Today you should volunteer at the homeless shelter." Rather, it's a matter of walking in fellowship with God. As you read, study, meditate on, and apply His Word each day, you'll find the needed wisdom for every opportunity.

Evangelist Anne Graham Lotz describes her strategy for success this way: "I just try to faithfully follow the Lord step-by-step and day-by-day. Ten years from now, I just want to look back . . . and know that to the best of my ability I have been obedient to God's call on my life."[12]

Serve Others Selflessly

Here's another clue in pursuing God's purpose for your life. You can be certain that in some way it will always involve serving others.

Earlier I talked about your uniqueness in the church, which is the body of Christ. But your work for the Lord extends beyond the walls of your church buildings. The purpose of the church is to prepare the followers of Christ to take the reality of the gospel to the whole world. We are all called to serve and to share with our lost and needy world. For me, this was a life-changing concept. I grew up in a pastor's home, but only later as a young adult did I really develop a biblical awareness of my responsibility to those who don't know Jesus Christ. That reality altered my life.

We can never truly find our purpose in life until we realize we're under orders to obey the Great Commission to "go into all the world and preach the gospel" (Mark 16:15). And the key to the Great Commission is the Great Commandment, which tells us to "love your neighbor as yourself" (Matt. 22:39).

A couple of years ago, Sam Sorenson sold a horse to Jennifer, a woman living in Montana. The two stayed in touch so Jennifer could keep Sam updated on the horse's status. Sam noticed that Jennifer had what so many people want—money, land, and freedom to live out her dreams. But she seemed lonely. Sam sensed she was using the horse to try to fill a void in her life.

Shortly afterward, Sam moved to Fort Worth to enroll in biblical studies at a seminary, and the two chatted by phone about his move. "She had some questions, but mostly she was looking for hope," Sam said. "I was able to ask her about some of her fears and hopes and then share my testimony. . . . I shared about how I came to faith in Jesus and told her what He has done for me."

Jennifer admitted she felt empty, and her dream of owning a horse hadn't filled that void as she had hoped. Sam asked if he could pray for her, and during the prayer Jennifer asked Jesus to come into her heart as her Lord and Savior.

"She is the first one I have shared the Gospel with who has accepted Jesus Christ as Lord and Savior," said Sam. "Praise the Lord."[13]

Yes, praise the Lord! As we serve others, we will find opportunities to share the gospel according to God's providence. This is part of His purpose for you. The greatest continuing joy of being a Christian is the joy of sharing Christ with others and then serving others in the body of Christ.

Experience Eternal Life

So let's sum up. You need a compelling motive if you're going to develop an unfolding plan for moving forward in your life. You need the *why*. You discover your why by totally presenting yourself to God and understanding that He has made you uniquely for a unique work. You have a God-given responsibility, and you need to actively pursue what's next on God's agenda for you. You'll need to stay in the Scripture daily and serve others selflessly, looking for opportunities to share the gospel.

And that brings us to the final step in pursuing your purpose: experience the eternal life God has given you.

Jesus said, "I have come that they may have life, and that they may have it more abundantly. . . . I give them eternal life, and they shall never perish; neither shall anyone snatch them out of My hand" (John 10:10, 28).

That's what everyone is looking for: the kind of life that is both abundant and eternal.

The Israeli statesman Abba Eban wrote about a conversation he had with Edmund Hillary, the first man to climb Mount Everest. Eban asked the explorer what he felt when he reached the peak. Hillary said the first sentiment was ecstatic accomplishment. But then there came a sense of desolation. What was there now left to do?[14]

Jon Krakauer trekked to the same summit years later, but the trip was tragic. Twelve of his companions were killed in the expedition. Later in his book *Into Thin Air*, Krakauer described how it felt at the top of Everest. "I'd been fantasizing about this moment, and the release of emotion that would accompany it, for many months. But now that I was finally here, actually standing on the summit of Mount Everest, I just couldn't summon the energy to care. . . . I snapped four quick photos . . . then turned and headed down. My watch read 1:17 P.M. All told, I'd spent less than five minutes on the roof of the world."[15]

Oh, if they only knew the truth of 1 John 5:12: "He who has the Son has life; he who does not have the Son of God does not have life."

God's ultimate purpose for us is to experience, enjoy, and embody the eternal life Jesus died to bestow on us. He fills our emptiness with Himself—and with His glorious will for each of us. He fills us with the certain hope of eternal life.

But let me ask you a question: When does eternal life begin? When you die?

No, you're living in eternal life the minute you believe. Jesus said, "Now this is eternal life: that they know you, the only true God, and Jesus Christ, whom you have sent" (John 17:3 NIV). Your eternal life begins the moment you put your trust in Jesus Christ. Did you know that? From that moment on, you will never die. When you accept Christ, you get life—both abundant and eternal.

When you find your purpose as a believer, that purpose isn't going to be realized wholly in this life on earth. Your life has eternity stamped on it, and it doesn't end if you should die before the return of Jesus Christ.

The apostle Paul said, "So we make it our goal to please him, whether we are at home in the body or away from it" (2 Cor. 5:9 NIV).

What you're doing today has eternal meaning. As you pursue your divine purpose, you'll increasingly see how this earthly world is connected to the heavenly world, which will be your home forever.

The only way meaning can come into your life is if someone outside your world brings it to you. Almighty God, realizing we were lost in our closed-system world of emptiness and chaos, put His hand on the shoulder of His perfect Son, Jesus Christ, and sent Him out of heaven into this world. And He said, "Go and give them life everlasting."

There was no other way. Almighty God is holy, absolutely and perfectly holy. He wants us to spend eternity with Him in heaven, but He couldn't bring us into His presence as sinful creatures. The only way He could bring us to heaven and satisfy His holiness and justice was to send Jesus Christ into the world. Jesus Christ took our sin upon Himself, bled and died, and was buried and rose again. He purchased for us a place in heaven.

He compressed the suffering of an entire world of humanity into the few hours that He suffered on the cross. It was suffering to a magnitude we'll never know.

To get out of emptiness and into purpose, you have to go through Jesus. He is the way, the truth, and the life. And when you receive Him as Savior, eternal life begins at that moment for you—and with it comes a life of purpose.

No Regrets!

It was impossible for me to write this chapter without thinking of a hero of mine—William Borden. He died before I was born, but his biography moved me like few other books, and I want to live by the six famous words famously attributed to him.

Borden grew up on Chicago's Gold Coast, where his family owned the Borden Dairy farm and business. He was a millionaire while in high school—and that was in the early 1900s when millionaires were few and far between. He was bright, good-looking, and athletic. He was also a young man who loved the Lord Jesus and had grown in Christ under the influence of his pastor, Dr. R. A. Torrey.

Borden's graduation present was a trip around the world, and that's where he developed a passion for spreading the gospel to the regions beyond, especially to China. Later at a missions conference he was deeply moved to give his entire life to spreading the gospel, including his fortune, which was valued at $50 million. Borden's family supported him in every way, and the day came when he left home and sailed to Egypt for language studies. Everyone who met him was charmed by his humility, his joy and love, and his passion for Christ. Yet within a month Borden contracted spinal meningitis. He lingered for two weeks, but passed away at the age of twenty-five.

The sacrifice wasn't wasted. Borden's story was proclaimed in newspapers around the world, in books and biographies, and from a thousand pulpits and lecterns. Even today, over a hundred years later, his story grips all who read it. No one knows how many young people, inflamed by his sacrifice, gave their lives to missions.

In his best-known biography, *Borden of Yale '09*, Mrs. Howard Taylor wrote, "No reserve, no retreat, no regrets had any place in Borden's consecration to God."[16]

No reserve! No retreat! No regrets! Many people believe those six words were inscribed in Borden's Bible, which has been lost to history. One thing we know for sure—they were certainly inscribed on his heart. That's the way he lived, and that's the only way to live.

You only have one life on earth. Since time doesn't move backward, you have a certain allocation of hours, days, or years left to you. Every one of them from this split second onward is in the future. There's no time to waste. You want to live every day without reservations, without retreating from the cause, and with no regrets when you're finished.

Chapter 7

Believe

Get Your Mind Right

Some meetings you'll never forget! When I was in New York a while ago, the hotel manager pulled me aside. He knew I loved sports and offered to introduce me to a fellow guest, Clemson football head coach Dabo Swinney, whose career I've long followed.

My family and I sat with Dabo for an hour as he talked about his faith, his love for football, his excitement about his players, and his zest for life. The love he had for his team was obvious. He was animated, speaking with his eyes and gesturing with his hands. I've seldom been around anyone more positive! I remember thinking, *No wonder he wins championships. He* is *a champion. He is a man who believes!*

Dabo's real name is William Christopher. He was born to a mother who battled debilitating polio. When he was a baby his older brother, Tripp, tried to call him "that boy," and Swinney was known as "Dabo" ever since. When Tripp was sixteen, a horrible accident left him permanently injured. About the same time, their father had business problems, fell into debt, and started drinking heavily. Dabo's parents broke up, and Dabo lived from pillar to post.

At sixteen, Dabo had a life-changing experience with Christ, and his newfound faith bolstered his belief in the future and in himself. He tried out for the University of Alabama football team as a walk-on and got a scholarship. During his last college game, on New Year's Day 1993, the Crimson Tide won the national championship. At the end of his college career, Dabo reconciled with his father and eventually helped lead him to Christ.[1]

In 2003, Dabo joined the coaching staff at Clemson. He became head coach in 2008. At the time, Clemson was known for losing games they should have won. It happened so often people called it "Clemsoning." Coach Swinney knew belief was at low ebb both inside and outside the program, so he posted a large sign in the training room bearing one word: *BELIEVE!*

The coach's belief was sincere—and contagious. No matter the challenges or setbacks, he believed in his players more than they believed in themselves. He believed in them so much their confidence surged, and under his leadership, the Tigers won national championships in 2016 and 2018.[2]

Part of my admiration for Coach Swinney comes from my own background. I grew up knowing a lot more about doubting than believing. I was raised in a good church, but it was better known for what it was *against* than what it was *for*. At the time, I didn't realize how that can affect one's outlook. To be sure, there are lots of things we *should* be against, but that mustn't be our primary focus. It took a while for me to learn that; but praise God I did, or there's no way I'd be doing what I'm now trying to do in the kingdom of God.

It takes a positive attitude to move forward. As you read that, you may be thinking, *Dr. Jeremiah is falling into the positive-thinking trap.* No, I'm not. I know about that pitfall. "Conceive it, believe it, achieve it!" "Health and wealth!" "Name it and claim it!" Lots of motivational speakers and self-help preachers make lots of promises without preaching the whole gospel—or any of it. The self-improvement indus-try has become a kind of religion that says, "If it's going to be, it's up to me." We should guard ourselves like Gideon against any self-help ideology that pushes God to the sidelines, magnifies human ability, and doesn't tell the whole truth.

But there is a positive, hopeful, joyful optimism that is totally biblical in its essence and comes from Christ alone. You can be a Christian and an optimist at the same time—and you should be. Faith adds a positive power to your life. Just listen to Philippians 4:13: "I can do all things through Christ who strengthens me."

That sounds pretty positive, doesn't it? The man who wrote those words was an Optimist with a capital O. Read his story in the book of Acts and study his thirteen letters. They're packed with optimism. Dr. John Henry Jowett said of Paul: "His eyes are always illumined. The cheery tone is never absent from his speech. The buoyant and springy movement of his life is never changed. The light never dies out of his sky. . . . The apostle is an optimist."[3]

We've seen that seizing the dreams God plants in your heart requires not only risk but also the willingness to pursue those dreams with abandon. Now I want to show you the importance of believing in the reality of those dreams—and yes, believing in yourself—in order to move forward.

So, for the next few minutes, sit at the feet of the great apostle and learn his powerful secrets for resilience, optimism, and positive belief. By stepping into his story at critical moments, you can understand how he lived a life of positive accomplishment despite hardships, which is the only way to plunge forward into the future God has for you.

Be Positive in Your Convictions

Paul's optimism started with his positive convictions. Travis Bradberry, the author of the bestselling book *Emotional Intelligence 2.0*, wrote, "When leaders have conviction, people's brains can relax, so to speak, letting them concentrate on what needs to be done. When people feel more secure in the future, they're happier and produce higher quality work."[4]

A conviction is a fixed belief, a deeply held set of certainties that lodges in the center of your mind and heart. It's critical that your convictions be sound and true. Paul's certainly were! He wrote them all down, and you can study them. His letters are a journal of his life, and his belief system is everywhere on display.

Paul's core convictions were the foundation of his incredible life and ministry. And here's the best part: you can embrace them for yourself, and they will provide powerful motivation and direction for your life.

Here are two examples of how to do just that as you move forward toward everything God has in store for the next phase of your life.

Be Positive About God's Love for You

The most basic conviction in life is rooted in understanding the nature of God. Without a good, powerful, loving, creative, eternal God, there's no basis for optimism.

Consider Paul's words in Romans 8:38–39: "For I am persuaded that neither death nor life, nor angels nor principalities nor powers, nor things present nor things to come, nor height nor depth, nor any other created thing, shall be able to separate us from the love of God which is in Christ Jesus our Lord." Consider the reasons for optimism packed into this passage. Not only is God real but He loves us. And not only does God love us, but nothing we might experience can separate us from His love.

Country music singer Carrie Underwood commented on this passage, "I love all the commas in these verses—neither death, nor life, nor angels, nor demons. It's so powerful."[5]

The ten things Paul lists in these verses could each be a potential barrier between you and God. But Paul says, with absolute assurance, that none of them can separate you from God's love.

The late John Stott, a brilliant pastor, wrote: "Nothing seems stable in our world any longer. Insecurity is written across all human experience. Christian people are not guaranteed immunity to temptation, tribulation, or tragedy, but we are promised victory over them. God's pledge is not that suffering will never afflict us. But that it will never separate us from His love."[6]

The loss of hope around us today is rampant, and it's lethal. It touches families all around our globe in ways hard to comprehend; and it stems from a growing ignorance or rejection of God's love.

The powerful words in Romans 8 about God's love are reinforced by a blessing Paul offered toward the end of that same book. It's become a favorite verse for many people I know, especially for those going through difficult times in their lives: "Now may the God of hope fill you with all joy and peace in believing, that you may abound in hope by the power of the Holy Spirit" (Rom. 15:13).

Take a moment to say that verse aloud three times right now—but make one little change. Turn it into a prayer that's personal to you: *Now may the God of hope fill me with all joy and peace in believing, so that I may abound in hope by the power of the Holy Spirit.*

May I suggest you pray those words aloud every morning, every noontime, and every evening until you know them by heart? That prayer can adjust your mindset in any given season of life, deepen your core convictions, and strengthen your belief—which is what Wendi Lou Lee discovered.

Wendi was the delightful child actor who played Grace Ingalls on the television series *Little House on the Prairie*. She's grown up now, and her life has taken some difficult twists, including a terrible health crisis. But she has a deep faith in God and a personal relationship with Jesus Christ. When Fox News interviewed her and asked how her health crisis impacted her, she said, "I just kept going back to that verse in Romans 15:13. . . . And after surgery, I was so joyful and so at peace—more than really made sense. And I think that's because I put my trust in God."[7]

I encourage you to make this a regular prayer—maybe for the next month or maybe for years to come: *Now may the God of hope fill me with all joy and peace in believing, so that I may abound in relentless hope by the power of the Holy Spirit.*

God loves you and wants you to overflow with hope and optimism! Never forget that. Let that conviction dwell in the very core of your being.

In his book *The Wisdom of Tenderness*, Brennan Manning tells the story of Edward Farrell, a man who decided to travel from his hometown of Detroit to visit Ireland, where he would celebrate his uncle's eightieth birthday. Early on the morning of his uncle's birthday, they went for a walk along the shores of Lake Killarney. As the sun rose, his uncle turned and stared straight into the breaking light. For twenty minutes they stood there in silence, and then his elderly uncle began to skip along the shoreline, a radiant smile on his face.

After catching up with him, Edward asked, "Uncle Seamus, you look very happy. Do you want to tell me why?"

"Yes, lad," the old man said, tears washing down his face. "You see, the Father is very fond of me. Ah, me Father is so very fond of me."

In the moment Uncle Seamus experienced how much he was loved by his Father in heaven, an overwhelming sense of joy flooded his heart. And he began to dance along the shoreline.[8]

Have you ever had a moment like that? Have you ever awakened and said, "He really does love me"? Do you know what it means to overflow with hope and optimism? Paul did, and you can too. Hope and optimism can become your habitual attitude.

Be Positive About God's Plan for You

That brings us to the second core conviction of biblically positive people—they're optimistic about their exciting future. Moving forward means embracing tomorrow with enthusiasm! That's only possible if you know your future is guaranteed to be exciting, eternal, meaningful, and useful. Only one Person can assure you of that—the

Lord Himself; and only one Book can provide the sure and certain details—the Bible.

The apostle Paul constantly referred to the future. He put the past behind him and strained forward toward what was ahead. Even when he was near death, Paul was excited about tomorrow. Think of it! While waiting on death row for his martyrdom, Paul was eager for tomorrow.

The last known letter Paul wrote was to his friend Timothy, and it was written from a Roman prison as he awaited a certain death. Listen to what he said in the final chapter of his final book: "For I am already being poured out as a drink offering, and the time of my departure is at hand. I have fought a good fight, I have finished the race, I have kept the faith. Finally, there is laid up for me the crown of righteousness, which the Lord, the righteous Judge, will give to me on that Day, and not to me only but also to all who have loved His appearing" (2 Tim. 4:6–8).

Paul had an incredible perspective on dying. Years before, he told the Philippians, "For to me, living means living for Christ, and dying is even better. But if I live, I can do more fruitful work for Christ. So I really don't know which is better. I'm torn between two desires: I long to go and be with Christ, which would be far better for me. But for your sakes, it is better that I continue to live" (Phil. 1:21–24 NLT).

Perhaps Paul's remarkable perspective flowed from the time he was caught up to heaven and glimpsed the glories that await us there (2 Cor. 12:4). But we have a blessing Paul didn't have: we have the book of Revelation, which was written after Paul's death, and the final two chapters describe our heavenly home in great detail for us (Rev. 21–22). The more we study those chapters, the more excited we become about tomorrow.

How long has it been since you were really excited about the future? When you went to bed last night, were you excited to see what today held? Remember when you were a kid counting the days till your birthday? Or a graduate looking forward to your next step in life? Or engaged to be married and eager for your wedding day? An expectant parent waiting for the baby to arrive? A hardworking adult excited about the cruise you planned?

In her book *Think Forward to Thrive*, Dr. Jennice Vilhauer wrote, "Although we often think the past dictates our behavior, the future is what really motivates most of our actions."[9]

There is an agelessness to optimists that keeps tomorrow fresh. One man who seems ageless is Dick Van Dyke. He's ninety-four, but he doesn't know it. In his book *Keep Moving*, he recalled filming a Disney movie. He was performing a dance scene when he suddenly felt the back of his leg snap like a rubber band. His injury grew worse, and he saw a doctor who took a bunch of X-rays.

After studying them intensely, the doctor looked at Van Dyke and said, "You're covered with arthritis from head to foot. I'm surprised you could dance. I've never seen so much arthritis in a single person."

"What about a married person?" asked Dick, ever the comedian.

"Married or single, you're literally suffused with arthritis," said the doctor.

"What about the pain in my leg?"

"It's the arthritis," the doctor answered, chiding him and telling him it was no joking matter. The doctor predicted Van Dyke would be using a walker if not a wheelchair within five years.

Dick was scared so badly he did something rash. He stood up in the examining room and started tapping his toes, then shuffling around, then dancing, "as if proving to myself I could still order my body to do a soft shoe anytime I wanted."

The doctor looked at him in shock.

"That was in 1967," said Dick. "I was forty years old. And I have not stopped moving ever since. Nor do I plan to hit the stop button anytime soon. . . . As a card-carrying the-glass-is-half-full optimist, I'm going to . . . declare that old age doesn't have to be a dreary weather report. In 99.9 percent of the stories I have heard it is better than the alternative, if only because you get to see what happens next. How can you not be curious?"[10]

As a follower of Christ, I'm ready to die and willing to live, but in either case I can't wait to see what God will do next. How can you not be curious? The Bible says, "For because of our faith, he has brought us into this place of highest privilege where we now stand, and we confidently and joyfully look forward to actually becoming all that God has had in mind for us to be" (Rom. 5:2 TLB).

In the interest of fitness, a subway station in Sweden transformed its stairs into a piano keyboard that actually plays notes as people take the musical stairs. The result? Over sixty percent more people used the stairs on any given day. What a joyful way to start the day!

Life is an uphill climb, and God isn't likely to take you to heaven in an elevator. But imagine the music of heaven playing with every forward step as you ascend into the future He has for you. Your spirit should always keep moving forward and dancing to the music.

Be Positive in Your Conversations

Now let's talk about talking. If you're positive in your core convictions, you'll become more positive in your daily conversations. In recent years, I've been working out with Todd Durkin at his gym, Fitness Quest 10. It's near my home in San Diego, and it's one of America's best gyms. Todd is more than a trainer. He's a dedicated Christian who speaks motivationally to large numbers of people. His upcoming book is entitled *Get Your Mind Right*. I'm not surprised by that title, because whenever someone walks into Todd's gym, they're greeted with a shout: "Get your mind right!"

I need it! Getting out of bed and heading to the gym is no easy task each day. But an uplifting greeting and a positive shout helps improve our spirits. In the book of Ruth, when the landowner Boaz went out each morning to check on the harvesters, he greeted them by shouting, "The LORD be with you!" And they answered him, "The LORD bless you!" (Ruth 2:4).

What a positive way to start the day!

Speak Positively to Yourself

Sometimes we have no one to encourage us at the break of day, so we have to speak to ourselves, saying something like: "This is the day the LORD has made; we will rejoice and be glad in it" (Ps. 118:24). Try saying that aloud with enthusiasm upon rising each day. It will make a difference.

Outside of praying, your most important words are the ones you say to yourself. These words are silent but significant. Pop psychologists call this positive self-talk, but I'm going to skip the trends and go straight to Scripture. My thesis, remember, involves Paul's example to us. So did Paul ever talk to himself?

He said he strove to "take captive every thought to make it obedient to Christ" (2 Cor. 10:5 NIV). He said, "For in my inner being I delight in God's law" (Rom. 7:22 NIV). He said, "I am not ashamed, for I know whom I have believed and am persuaded that He is able to keep what I have committed to Him until that Day" (2 Tim. 1:12). And as we've learned, he also said, "I can do all things through Christ who strengthens me" (Phil. 4:13).

I recall preaching a sermon on how to handle negative thoughts, and I still remember my outline: *Don't curse them; Don't nurse them; Don't rehearse them; Disperse them.* That's still a good formula! Push out your negative thoughts—worry, anxiety, fear, pessimism—by filling your mind with God's Scripture, especially His promises. And then preach those promises to yourself.

Several years ago, I noticed my eyelids beginning to droop. It's a condition called *ptosis,* and the surgery that corrects it is called *blepharoplasty.* The only good thing about it is impressing others with the new medical terms you can pronounce. A friend recommended Dr. James Gills of St. Petersburg, Florida. Donna and I flew down for the surgery and were pleased to meet Dr. Gills and to learn he was a believer who listened to my sermons on the radio.

I was also surprised to learn that Dr. Gills was president of the Iron-Man Association and a world-class athlete. He'd completed a double triathlon (two triathlons back-to-back with only a twenty-four hour break) six times—the last time at age fifty-nine. When asked how he did it, he said, "I've learned to talk to myself instead of listening to myself. If I listen to myself, I hear all the reasons why I should give up. I hear that I'm too tired, too old, too weak to make it. But if I talk to myself, I can give myself the encouragement and words I need to hear to keep running and finish the race."

In Psalm 42 the psalmist said to himself, "Why are you cast down, O my soul? And why are you disquieted within me? Hope in God; for I shall yet praise Him, the help of my countenance and my God" (v. 11).

We don't know the author of Psalm 42, but it might have been King David, because he knew how to preach to himself when needed. As a younger man, a series of disastrous problems had befallen David in a town called Ziklag. His family and the families of his men had been kidnapped, and even his own men were turning on him and talking about stoning him to death.

What did David do? He preached to himself. He "strengthened himself in the LORD his God" (1 Sam. 30:6). And in that strength he rose up to tackle his problems with a positive spirit that came from his belief in God's watchful care of his life.

Jeremiah did the same. After watching his city go up in flames and his nation go down in defeat, he said in Lamentations 3:21–23: "This I recall to my mind, therefore I have hope. Through the LORD's mercies we are not consumed, because His compassions fail not. They are new every morning; great is Your faithfulness."

This is what we must do. If we listen to the negative tapes looping around in our thoughts, we'll sink into the pessimism of the devil. *How could I have been so stupid? What's wrong with me? Everything is falling apart. This is a disaster. Why is this happening to me?*

Stop the tape! Here's a better one: *I know in Whom I believe, and I am persuaded He is able to keep what I have entrusted to Him. Why are you cast down? Hope in God. I'll soon be praising Him again, for He is the health of my countenance. I'm going to recall something and keep it in mind—the Lord is merciful, and His compassions won't fail me. They are new every morning. Great is His faithfulness. I can do all things through Christ who strengthens me.*

"We're constantly processing thoughts," wrote Dr. H. Norman Wright. "Depending on how active your mind is, you may produce more than 45,000 thoughts a day. Whew! It might be compared to a flock of birds flying in and out of your mind."

To complicate our minds more, noted Dr. Wright, not all these are conscious thoughts, and sometimes they pass so fleetingly we barely notice them. But listen to what Dr. Wright says next: "Every time you have a thought, it triggers an electrochemical reaction in your body . . . Each thought sets off a biological process—about 400 billion at once. Because of that thought, chemicals surge through the body, producing electromagnetic waves. Those set off emotions, which affect how we behave. . . . Science simply confirms what Scripture has been saying all along: We are shaped, in large part, by our thoughts."[11]

Speak Positively to Others

Learn to talk to yourself instead of listening to yourself. Learn to preach to yourself. Learn to encourage yourself in the Lord. It will change the way you speak to others. Your mood and message will be different, even in the midst of difficulties.

This was another of Paul's secrets. Once he was caught in a vicious storm with a terrified crew on a sinking ship. The typhoon threatened to rip the ship into matchsticks, and even the captain gave up hope of survival. But Paul rallied their spirits, saying, "Keep up your courage, men, for I have faith in God" (Acts 27:25 NIV).

Nevertheless the storm grew worse. It was the deadliest storm the sailors had ever seen, and there were 276 souls on board. Two weeks of unbearable strain drained the crew of their last drops of hope, and none of them could eat or rest through the wild hours of the worst night.

"Just before dawn, Paul urged them all to eat. 'For the last fourteen days,' he said, 'you have been in constant suspense and have gone without food—you haven't eaten anything. Now I urge you to take up some food. You need it to survive. Not one of you will lose a single hair from his head.' After he said this, he took some bread and gave thanks to God in front of them all. Then he broke it and began to eat. They were all encouraged" (Acts 27:33–36 NIV).

Do you know someone struggling to keep their head above water? Think of the power of saying to them—in the right way at the right time—"Keep up your courage! I have faith in God. Take care of yourself. You'll get through this storm. Believe God and His Word."

Oh, the power of an attitude that is positively biblical—and biblically positive.

Rabbi Joseph Telushkin has lectured around the country on the power of our words to either hurt or heal. He often asks his audience if they can go twenty-four hours without saying anything unkind to or about someone else. Most of the time, a few people will say yes but the others will admit that they can't.

Telushkin responds: "All of you who can't answer yes must recognize how serious a problem you have. Because if I asked you to go for twenty-four hours without drinking liquor, and you said, 'I can't do that,' I'd tell you, 'Then you must recognize you're an alcoholic.'. . . .Similarly, if you can't go twenty-four hours without saying unkind words about others, then you've lost control over your tongue."[12]

As London recovered from World War II, a prominent minister, Leslie Weatherhead, wrote a book to help his British congregation recover from the emotional trauma of the conflict. He warned his people to avoid talking all the time about what was wrong with them. We all need a very few close friends, of course, to whom we can unburden our hearts and share our troubles, he said. But telling everyone we meet about our troubles gives our woes "persisting power." It's tempting to share our difficulties, because we crave sympathy. "But we must realize that every recital of our woes and every brooding hour etches on our minds the picture of the weaker, not the stronger, self."[13]

The more we talk about our troubles, the more we rehearse and reinforce them, and the more we spread the pessimism that's endemic to our culture. Instead, focus on others. Spread optimism. Help those around you to take courage. Help them believe. Ephesians 4:29 advises, "Let everything you say be good and helpful, so that your words will be an encouragement to those who hear them" (NLT).

On a cold January day in 1990, a Boeing 707 with 159 passengers crashed on a remote, wooded hillside in Long Island. The plane broke into two sections, and the nose of the aircraft rested on the deck of a terrified elderly couple's home. The scene was almost indescribable, with debris everywhere, oxygen masks hanging on trees, people screaming, babies crying, and fear that the aircraft could burst into flames at any moment. Emergency responders, nearby neighbors, and local volunteers rushed to the scene and began trying to rescue survivors. Ordinary citizens worked alongside police officers and physicians to pull people from the aircraft, separate the living from the dead, and save the lives of the injured. One of the rescuers was Joan Imhof, who later described the strain of the scene that unfolded hour after hour.

Joan remembered a strange, strengthening camaraderie that instantly united the workers: "People would pass each other, reach and take a hand for a moment. Or they would look at each other, make a brief comment, and then move on. Sometimes they would embrace or nod, then continue applying bandages or moving bodies to a makeshift morgue. People needed that brief, but meaningful contact to continue working with determination. It rejuvenated us."[14]

Our world is wrecked, and as we work together to accomplish what God wants us to do, the last thing we need are endless critics. Instead, we need the camaraderie of Christ-centered people who say what is good and helpful so our words will be an encouragement to many. We need people who believe and who inspire belief.

Be Positive in Your Crises

Only after you've learned to be positive in your convictions and in your conversation can you learn to persevere with a hopeful attitude through challenges that will inevitably come.

Those challenges came several years ago to murder mystery writer Linda C. DeFew, who was diagnosed with TMJ and rheumatoid arthritis, forcing her into surgeries and out of her job as a law school secretary. She began keeping a journal, and as she thumbed through it she saw all her negative thoughts in pen and ink. "Dwelling on my problems would only make me worse," she told herself. So as difficult as it seemed, she began finding things to be grateful for—and there were a lot of them.

She wrote, "In my Bible studies I was influenced by the wisdom of King Solomon. He said we had two choices: Live a cheerful life and enjoy good health or allow a broken spirit to dry up our bones. I decided to go with his first suggestion. I began that day to accept my disability and vowed to go on with my life. To make it work, I had to do away with negative thinking. My decision to think positive led to positive actions."

Linda went back to college at age forty, using the eraser of a big fat pencil to pound out letters on her keyboard. She read every story she could find about people who overcame insurmountable obstacles. She read her Bible and other wisely chosen self-help books and decided to start writing her own columns and stories.

"I noticed I was smiling more, even when I didn't feel like it. I formed friendships with people who had their own challenges to overcome. . . . Instead of dwelling on what I couldn't do, I woke up each morning with a welcome wave of optimism. Despite my handicap, I was seeing each day as an opportunity to move forward."[15]

During times of conflict and crisis, optimism shines through like the sun piercing storm clouds. That was true for our hero, the resilient Paul. He said in Romans 8:35–37: "Who shall separate us from the love of Christ? Shall tribulation, or distress, or persecution, or famine, or nakedness, or peril, or sword? As it is written: 'For Your sake we are killed all day long; we are accounted as sheep for the slaughter.' Yet in all these things we are more than conquerors through Him who loved us."

The apostle lists seven persecutions he had constantly endured. It felt like "being killed all day long." But he said he was "more than a conqueror."

The phrase *more than conquerors* is the translation of a Greek word: *hypernikomen*. Notice the letters "nik" are in the middle of the word—*hypernikomen*. *Nike* is the Greek word for victory, which is why a great company chose it for its title. It means overcomer. And look at the first part of the term—hyper*nikomen*. You know the term *hyper*. It means extra, obsessive, over and above. So the phrase *more than conquerors* is a super-term. It means super-overcomer. Paul didn't just overcome his difficulties. He kept overcoming them again and again through the power of Him who loved him—the Lord Jesus Christ.

We can't control everything that happens to us, and we have little say-so in the affairs of this world. But we can choose our response to what happens—we can mope, cope, or hope. I'm here to tell you that biblical hope is the greatest source of optimism in the world. It's relentless, rewarding, and the essence of personal revival.

Back in the early nineties, someone gave me a book by Martin Seligman called *Learned Optimism*. Over the years I've read that book numerous times, and it's as marked up and dog-eared as any book I have. Dr. Seligman said,

> The optimists and the pessimists: I have been studying them for twenty-five years. The defining characteristic of pessimists is that they tend to believe bad events will last a long time, will undermine everything they do, and are their own fault.
>
> The optimists, who are confronted with the same hard knocks of this world, think about misfortune in the opposite way. They tend to believe defeat is just a temporary setback, and it's causes are confined to this one case. . . . Such people are unfazed by defeat. Confronted by a bad situation, they perceive it as a challenge and try harder.[16]

In other words, if you want to know if you're an optimist or a pessimist, trouble and difficulty will help you sort it out. Let's sort it out like Linda C. DeFew did. Let's sort it out like the apostle Paul did.

I want to shout through the pages of this book to you: on the authority of Scripture and because of the love of Jesus Christ, be an over-the-top overcomer. Believe! Trust Him! And be positive in your convictions, your conversations, your crises, and finally in your countenance.

Be Positive in Your Countenance

Remember how Linda DeFew said, "I noticed I was smiling more, even when I didn't feel like it"? Your mood is always reflected in your countenance. When optimism is in your heart, a joyful countenance is on your face. Someone said, "What's down in the well comes up in the pail." Let me quote Psalm 42 once again: "Hope in God; for I shall yet praise Him, the help of my countenance and my God" (v. 11).

Unfortunately, I don't have a photograph of the apostle Paul, so

I can't prove his face was radiant, but who can doubt it? His smile and positive attitude infiltrated his writings. For example, he told the Corinthians, "And we all, who with unveiled faces contemplate the Lord's glory, are being transformed into his image with ever-increasing glory, which comes from the Lord, who is the Spirit" (2 Cor. 3:18 NIV).

According to the Association for Psychological Science, a University of Kansas study found an incredible link between smiling and the ability to recover from difficult episodes in life. Did you know there are two kinds of smiles? There are standard smiles, which use the muscles around the mouth. And there are genuine (or Duchenne) smiles, which engage the muscles around both your mouth and eyes. The real key is your eyes.

Why not try it right now? First, practice smiling with your mouth, and then give it a try with your mouth and eyes. Can you feel the difference?

In the study, participants were subjected to stressful tasks, like submerging their hands in frigid water. Some were told to smile, and others were given chopsticks to hold in their teeth so they couldn't smile. The results showed those who were told to smile—and especially those who smiled with their eyes—had a lower physical response to the stress, a higher degree of happiness, and a quicker rate of recovery.[17]

This might be the simplest advice you've ever heard: become an expert in Duchenne smiles! Over the years, I've read many books about sharing one's faith, but I've never read about the evangelistic power of a genuine smile.

Long before psychologists studied Duchenne smiles, the psalmist said, "They looked to Him and were radiant, and their faces were not ashamed" (Ps. 34:5). Ecclesiastes 8:1 says, "A person's wisdom brightens their face and changes its hard appearance" (NIV).

That inner wisdom comes from believing. It's not believing in positive thinking or the power of a positive attitude. It isn't even believing in ourselves. True optimism comes from deep biblical convictions about the nature of God, knowing He loves you and has an exciting plan that is uniquely yours. It comes from quoting Scripture to yourself and reminding yourself and others of His goodness and of the incredible future He has for those who trust Him. A firm belief in the God of Scripture will bear you through the crises of life and put joy on your face, unmatched by the world's best makeup. Your faith makes you radiant.

Stay Positive!

One day John Mason and his wife decided to have a cup of coffee at their local IHOP. Their server that day was a cheerful woman who smiled constantly with a radiant face. They noticed she wore a button that said, "A smile is a gift you can give every day." They also noticed she had only one tooth. John complimented her on the button and sincerely told her she had a bright smile, and he wondered if anyone had ever told her that before.

When the woman returned to their table with coffee, she explained that her father had done the calligraphy on the button. "He had his fingers cut off in an industrial accident," she said, "and then decided to pick up calligraphy after that!"

In recalling the story, John said, "Perhaps only a woman raised by a fingerless dad who does calligraphy can choose to smile even though she has only one tooth."

Then he added some wise advice: "A smile is an asset; a frown is a liability. Some people grin and bear it; others smile and change it. Being happy and enthusiastic is always a choice. . . . Both enthusiasm and pessimism are contagious. How much of each do you spread?"[18]

In November 2007, a tough old Alaska fisherman named Alan Ryden took a month-long trip at sea in his forty-two-foot boat. The trip became a nightmare when the boat capsized in a terrible storm.

Ryden managed to get into a raft wearing his survival suit and fleece jacket, and he got off a Mayday signal to the Coast Guard. But the weather was wicked, and the little raft tossed around like a cork.

Shivering in the buffeted raft, Alan felt himself losing hope. His mind panicked and quickly sunk into deep discouragement and hopelessness. He began wondering if his life insurance would provide for his family. Suddenly, Alan realized his own thoughts were pulling him under more than the seas, and he made one of the toughest decisions of his life. He determined to cast out negative thoughts and to toss them out of the raft like weights.

He began quoting Scripture to himself, speaking God's Word aloud. He started thanking God for any good thing that came to mind. He said to himself, "Well, at least I am in a survival suit. My suit does have a top-of-the-line strobe light attached. . . . At least I am in some kind of raft, and at least I got that fleece jacket on. . . . I am strong, a good swimmer, and have no fear of the water."

Ryden's mental struggle deepened as the darkness set in, but he remained committed to hanging on with all his strength to the anchor of hope. He later said, "There was definitely a grace from God. . . . I had to fight for every inch in my thoughts."

Ten hours later, Ryden was rescued. Tracie Miles, who wrote about his story in her book *Unsinkable Faith*, said the real rescue was inward. It had been achieved during the storm when, by grace, Ryden had "anchored himself in God and embraced positive thoughts, which helped him stay buoyant."

She's right. Believing and learning to be optimistic requires us to stay positive in our convictions, even amid our crises. It's an essential skill you must develop if you want to move forward in life. Therefore, I implore you: anchor yourself in the hope of Jesus Christ, cling to the promises of the Bible, and determine by God's grace to keep your mind buoyant and your soul unsinkable, even in the storms.

Chapter 8

Invest

Outlive Your Life

Not far from my home is a little black-and-white shop called See's Candies. They have amazing displays of chocolates. Over two hundred of these stores dot California and a few other states, along with hundreds of kiosks in airports and malls.

The chain was started in the 1920s when a Canadian couple named Charles and Florence See moved to California. Charles's widowed mother, Mary, came along, too, toting a handful of treasured candy recipes. The See family opened their first candy store in Los Angeles in November 1921.

The See family sold its business a few years ago—and guess who bought it? No, the new owner wasn't named Hershey or Nestle. It was Warren Buffet and his Berkshire Hathaway conglomerate. Buffet paid $25 million for See's Candies, and since then the return for his investment has topped more than $1.35 billion. Buffett has called See's one of the top investments he ever made.

Well, with due respect to Warren Buffet, the sweetest investments in the world don't come in assorted boxes of nuts and chews, nor in stock portfolios, nor in Wall Street transactions. The best expenditure you'll ever make is the legacy of a well-invested life.

We do need to take care of whatever physical and financial assets the Lord gives to us, whether it's a hundred dollars or a million dollars. If you know Jesus as Savior, all you have is His. He has entrusted it into your management, and stewarding it well is important for a financially secure future.

Proverbs 13:11 says, "Whoever gathers money little by little makes it grow" (NIV). And Proverbs 27:23 says, "Be sure you know the condition of your flocks, give careful attention to your herds" (NIV).

Few of us are shepherds or ranchers now, but the Bible's point is to be attentive and astute over whatever resources God has entrusted to us. As much as possible, we should be wary of debt, restrain spending, save prudently, invest wisely, and give generously.

The Bible talks about investing for both time *and* eternity—providing a legacy that will outlive us on earth and eternal returns that will never fade in heaven. No matter how well you invest on earth, if you aren't involved in the long-term investments of eternity, you're pouring all your resources into short-term ventures.

Someone once said, "The real measure of our wealth is how much we would be worth if we lost all our money."

Let me give you an incredible example of that principle in the story of Austin Carlile.

When Austin was fifteen, his parents divorced, and he felt ripped apart. He went to live with his mother, but within two years she died from an aneurysm caused by Marfan syndrome, a rare genetic disorder. Austin literally threw up his hands and cursed God. He turned to music. He said, "I had all this rage. A lot of it was toward God. I could yell into a mic and get all of that rage and hate out."

Austin started a band called Of Mice and Men, which took off like a rocket. They had hit after hit, and Austin raked in the money.

Sadly, he also inherited his mom's genetic disorder and began facing incredible pain. Alcohol and drug use took over his life. One day after a show he climbed on the roof of his touring bus, called his father, and said, "What am I missing? What am I doing wrong? I'm depressed. I'm in pain. My band is building this success, but I feel so empty and hurt and lost."

His father asked a simple question: "Where is God in your life?"

That question sent Austin to the Bible, and he finally prayed, "God, I want to come back." Even as he made a spiritual turnaround, his health continued to deteriorate, causing him to give up life on the road. He put all his belongings into a storage facility and moved to Costa Rica to be near his dad.

The rent on his storage facility was paid by monthly drafts to his credit card, but when the card expired without his knowledge, the storage facility cleaned out his unit and sold all his belongings.

"It was filled with everything that I ever owned," Austin said. "Everything that I had from childhood. I had my vinyl collection there, my recording equipment. I even had my mother's ashes in that unit."

He was left with only three suitcases of belongings.

Recently Austin sat down with author Doug Bender and said, "I still don't have anything. I don't have a job. I don't know what's next. I don't know what God is planning. But I have so much more joy, peace, and happiness now than I've had in my entire life. God showed me that everything I need is in Him. I literally have nothing else."[1]

In order to move forward toward God's plan for the next phase of your life, you'll need a dream. You'll need prayer. You'll need to set the right priorities, focus on the right goal, and take the right kinds of risks. You'll need to pursue your dreams with enthusiasm and believe in those dreams with optimism.

In addition to all that, you'll need the kind of wealth that will survive loss, and the kind of investments that will never become insolvent. That's the power of investing in an eternal legacy.

To do that, you'll have to determine which assets are eternal in essence—things that will never cease to exist. Moving forward means pouring yourself into those pursuits.

May I suggest three of them?

Invest in God's Word

First, make investments in God's Word. Psalm 119:89 says, "Your word, LORD, is eternal; it stands firm in the heavens" (NIV).

Many people long for more education, but it's a pricey venture. One of the most critical issues for our economy today is student debt. The cost of education has skyrocketed, and the amount of student debt some young people bear is daunting. But it's not just young people. It's not even *primarily* young people. Do you know the fastest-growing group of college loan debtors? It's Americans over the age of sixty!

It's not that retirees have old student debts of their own, though a few do. Nor are many going back to school, though some do. No, the reason is simple. Senior adults are borrowing money so their children and grandchildren can afford an education. In all, 2.8 million Americans over the age of sixty are contending with student debt.[2]

I don't know how to advise you on student debt because everyone's case is different. But I have one thing to say: education is important, but the most important school is absolutely free—the school of the Bible.

Think of God offering free scholarships to anyone who wants to study His Word! The wisest people on earth are those who are students of God's Word. All you need is a willingness to open its pages each day, pray for insight, and learn how to study it. The time you spend in God's Word is an investment in both eternal and internal wisdom.

Peter said, "'All flesh is as grass, and all the glory of man as the flower of the grass. The grass withers, and its flower falls away, but the word of the LORD endures forever.' Now this is the word which by the gospel was preached to you" (1 Pet. 1:24–25).

Jesus said, "Heaven and earth will pass away, but My words will by no means pass away" (Matt. 24:35).

The Bible is God's wisdom, and God's truth will never cease. Since we hold in our hands an eternal book, we'd better invest ourselves in it. How? There's a twofold method of investing in God's ceaseless Word.

Study His Word

Paul said, "Be diligent to present yourself approved to God, a worker who does not need to be ashamed, rightly dividing the word of truth" (2 Tim. 2:15).

When Ross McCall first came to Christ, he rode the bus to work every day with his head buried in his pocket Bible, underlining passages as they jumped off the page to him. He memorized verses, studied from different translations, and purchased commentaries to build his own Bible study library. But somewhere along the way, he became busier and busier, and his Bible study habits fell off.

"The Bible and I drifted apart," he said. "I'd open that same pocket Bible, but the connection to its contents was gone. We'd stopped talking to each other."

Then he was asked to teach a class on how to study the Bible. After he accepted, he began to panic. Some nights he woke up crying. "How could I impart enthusiasm for reading Scripture when I had stopped enjoying the Bible myself?"

As a result, he found ways to reengage with the Bible and how to teach others to do the same.[3]

What if you were asked to teach a "How to Study the Bible" course? Have you developed your habits well enough to show someone how to do it? Or have you and your Bible drifted apart?

Believe me, you can do a lot with a Bible, a pencil or pen, and fifteen minutes. Start in one of the Gospels or epistles, and read consecutively day after day, marking the things you notice and appreciate. Start with as little as five minutes a day, but do it consistently. Read, mark, and pray. I have a feeling the five minutes will easily grow to an enriching hour.

The Bible gives us eternal information from heaven for life on earth, and there's no better investment on earth than the time you spend every day soaking in its truths. We invest a lot of time today on our electronic devices, social media, and computer games. What would happen if you devoted a portion of that time to serious Bible study? It would build you into a person with the essential skills needed to face these days.

On my new phone I have noticed that if I push the right button, I get a report on how much time I spent on the phone the day before. I wonder what would happen if we had a way to report how much time we spend in the Word of God each day. I'm afraid some of us would disable the app.

Spread His Word

There's another way we invest in God's Word: by spreading it. Whenever you give away a Bible or a New Testament—or whenever you support someone who does—you're investing in eternity.

Have you heard of Jack Murphy? He was one of the most notorious jewel thieves in American history. He was a gifted man on many levels—a musician, an actor, an artist, a surfer. He was born in Oceanside, California; then his family moved to Pittsburgh, where he played violin with the Pittsburgh Symphony Orchestra and also won a tennis scholarship to the University of Pittsburgh.

Unknown to everyone, he was also a cat burglar. On October 29, 1964, he pulled off one of the greatest heists in American history, stealing twenty-four precious gems from J. P. Morgan's prized collection at the American Museum of Natural History in New York. The stolen gems included the Star of India, the Eagle Diamond, and the DeLong Star Ruby.

Three days later, Murphy and his accomplices were arrested. The story goes from bad to worse, and Murphy ended up sentenced to 2,244 years in prison. One day some men came to minister to the prisoners. Football stars Bill Glass and Roger Staubach shared the gospel with Murph the Surf, as he was known, and he was intrigued.

Later a Christian worker who faithfully visited the prison followed up with a personal message from Scripture, and Murphy gave his life to Christ. Murphy was eventually released, and in the years since he's visited hundreds of prisons with the message of the gospel. His story was written up as part of a book called *God's Prison Gang*.[4]

The story doesn't end there. In California, a man named Mike Larson grew up in an abusive home, which led to an unstable life. He became enslaved to raging drug abuse. He lost every job and every meaningful relationship. One day he broke into a doctor's house looking for drugs, and he was arrested and thrown into prison.

While Mike was in solitary confinement, a prison guard handed him a book entitled *God's Prison Gang*, featuring stories of prisoners who came to Christ while behind bars. As Mike read Jack Murphy's story, he decided to leave his life of crime forever.

Upon his release, Mike decided to get a tattoo. The artist drawing the tattoo invited Mike to church with him and also urged Mike to join his motorcycle gang—but there was an unusual requirement. You had to bring along a biker vest with a notepad, a pen, and a pocket Bible.

When Mike lost his Bible, he tried to hide the fact he didn't have one. But it bothered him so much that one day he literally yelled out to God to give him a Bible.

Later that day Mike drove to a pizza restaurant where a man got out of his car, came over, and gave him a Bible—just like that, and then drove away. The man was a Gideon, and then and there Mike broke down in tears. He couldn't believe God had answered his prayer, and that led to his giving his heart totally to Jesus Christ.

Today Mike is a California pastor leading his church to invest itself in winning others to Christ.[5]

Think of the chain reaction: from famous athletes, to a diamond thief, to a prison guard, to a tattoo artist, to a nameless Gideon—a golden chain that's still forging new links every day.

When we share the Scriptures, we're like advisors helping people make the greatest investment in their lives. Matthew 13:44 says, "The kingdom of heaven is like treasure hidden in a field, which a man found and hid; and for joy over it he goes and sells all that he has and buys that field."

The apostle Paul said, "I consider everything a loss because of the surpassing worth of knowing Christ Jesus my Lord, for whose sake I have lost all things. I consider them garbage, that I may gain Christ" (Phil. 3:8 NIV).

Can you think of a better way to invest your life than by studying and spreading God's wisdom and His Word? Ask God how you can be part of it. I have a friend who ordered fifty pocket New Testaments, and whenever he's on a trip he keeps some of them in his carry-on luggage and offers them to fellow travelers, ride-share drivers, hotel bellhops, and others. Only heaven will reveal the results of this eternal investment.

Invest in God's Work

That leads to another step in God's strategy. Let's invest our time and abilities in His work on earth. The work of God is eternal—we'll still be serving Him in heaven (Rev. 22:3). His enterprise will never go bankrupt, and His servants will never be laid off. We're to serve Him as best we can until our last breath, and then we'll pick up where we left off and keep serving Him in heaven. God's work will never go out of business.

So let's begin now—right where we are. Here are two specific ways you can invest in God's work.

Develop a Personal Ministry

From God's perspective, life is defined by serving. Jesus said, "The Son of Man did not come to be served, but to serve" (Matt. 20:28).

Do you know how many ways we can serve? At least 7.7 billion, because that's the estimated population of earth, and every person has a need.

Think of your time and abilities. What can you do for the Lord?

Jesus said, "No one can serve two masters; for either he will hate the one and love the other, or else he will be loyal to the one and despise the other. You cannot serve God and [money]" (Matt. 6:24).

Jesus invested His life in service, and He longs for us to do the same. Romans 7:4 says, "So, my dear brothers and sisters, this is the point: You died to the power of the law when you died with Christ. And now you are united with the one who was raised from the dead. As a result, we can produce a harvest of good deeds for God" (NLT).

Patrick Morley wrote about his friend Owen, who has a lucrative business leasing commercial real estate. For decades, Owen has also led a Monday noon Bible study in downtown Orlando. Owen has also been instrumental in helping several new churches get started. One day someone asked him, "Why don't you go into the ministry?"

Owen said, "I am in the ministry. God has called me to business."

In telling that simple story, Morley rightly observed, "We don't need to be in occupational ministry to serve God. A few may be called to occupational ministry, but 99% of us will minister through our jobs, families, church involvements, and community activities. . . . God's plan is for every believer to have a personal ministry."[6]

Do you know the word *ministry* simply means "service"?

God hasn't placed you on earth for a few fleeting decades to serve yourself but to serve Him and those He brings near you. He has given you a unique set of gifts and talents. Your primary task here is to invest yourself in the personal ministry God has for you.

And think of this—everything you've ever experienced in your life, good and bad, has prepared you for what's ahead. God has a unique area of service just for you, and that service is part of His plan for you as you move forward.

That's what Bill Brantley of Pensacola discovered. He's been riding a bicycle since he was four years old. He estimates he put one hundred thousand miles on his twenty-six-inch boyhood bike, and he learned how to fix it whenever the chain broke or the screws came loose. In time, he learned how to take bicycles apart, repair them, replace parts, and put them back together.

Bill is eighty-seven years old now, and his personal ministry is— bicycles. His local church has a ministry to the homeless, and one day Bill brought a couple of restored bicycles to the church, wondering if someone might need one. Soon everyone was bringing their old bicycles to him as a donation. Now Bill spends hours in his garage each day, repairing old bicycles and getting them in good shape. Each one goes to someone in need and is distributed by his church. Bill and his wife, Patsy, often hear the recipient say something like, "Boy, I can get back and forth to my work every day. I sure do appreciate that bike."[7]

Here's another personal ministry that operates out of a garage. One day Chris Williams of Texas noticed a woman and child walking on the highway in the rain. He stopped to offer them a ride and learned they were members of the church he attended. "They told me that their car had been in the shop for months," Chris said, "and they couldn't afford to get it out. Right then, I decided that I needed to figure out a way to get my dream of opening a free garage off the ground."

Williams, a former children's pastor, borrowed money, solicited donations, and recruited volunteers. Today God's Garage is a non-profit auto repair shop that helps single mothers, widows, and the wives of deployed military members. They repair cars and accept donated ones, which they overhaul for someone who needs them. That's not all. They also conduct seminars for women who receive their cars, in which they teach life skills and values.

Chris said, "My dad went to tech school to become a mechanic before he became a pastor, and I followed him into the pastor side of things, but didn't know much about cars. My dad taught me the basics of car care, and I grew up watching him help people stuck on the side of the road. As I grew older, I kept telling myself, 'When I'm in the right position, I'm going to help people.' So when I saw this need in my community, I decided the solution was to surround myself with guys who know more about fixing cars than I do. Together, we're making it happen at God's Garage."[8]

Now, if you can't fix bicycles or cars, don't worry. Just look around at your life. What are you doing? What do you enjoy doing? What are you good at doing? Who is near you? Do you see people with needs?

Take an inventory of all that, then say, "Lord, You have made me usable, so show me how You want to use me!"

When you find an area of personal ministry and begin serving the Lord in the simple but wonderful way He gives you, you'll never suffer boredom. Whether God gives you a ministry of prayer, of writing letters, of visiting nursing homes, of raising grandchildren, or of evangelizing prostitutes—you'll be investing in a divine enterprise that will never file for Chapter 11.

Devote Yourself to a Local Church

But while we're each called to invest ourselves in a personal ministry, we're not isolated entities when it comes to the Lord's work. Romans 12:4–5 says, "For just as each of us has one body with many members, and these members do not all have the same function, so in Christ we, though many, form one body, and each member belongs to all the others" (NIV).

When Christ returned to heaven, He left behind one and only one great organism for continuing His work: His church. And His church is eternal. It isn't made of bricks and mortar but of human beings— living stones. We're His family, and He has made us part of the family business.

Trudy Smith discovered the truth about this. She grew up in a family that valued regular church attendance, and even when she headed off to college she found a local church and maintained the habit of attending every weekend. But as time went by, she became so involved in ministries on the street that she neglected church attendance. In fact, she grew cynical toward the church.

"I followed Jesus right out of the church and into the streets, communing with homeless people over slices of pizza and hearing sermons in the words of the people who lived in the shelter on skid row. . . . It occurred to me that perhaps what was more important than how often I showed up for a Sunday service was how often I showed up for people who were in need."

Trudy grew frustrated with churches that didn't share her passion for alleviating poverty.

"But then another strange thing happened," she said. "I kept following Jesus, and eventually, He led me right back into church. I was surprised."

Trudy came to realize that the church wasn't an exclusive club for people who thought themselves superior. "It was more like a refuge where all sorts of people could gather to remind each other of the story we were all in—the one about how God loves us, and is renewing our world and our souls in spite of all the damage that's been done."

Trudy said, "It wasn't perfect—sometimes I felt frustrated, bored or hurt—but it was good, and God was in it. Yes, church people could be apathetic, judgmental, and selfish—but so could I. And just like everybody else, I needed to be welcomed and loved anyway."

One day an older lady asked Trudy and her husband to be in charge of finding people to serve communion each week. "Now that we've shouldered even just this tiny bit of responsibility," she said, "we recognize how many people have to show up consistently to create the prayerful, welcoming, worshipful space we experience each week."

"It is an opportunity . . . to encounter, even when I least expect it, God in the midst of the people who are in my church."[9]

Moving forward toward God's plan for the next phase of your

life means investing yourself in eternal ventures. But I honestly don't think you can go forward if you leave the church behind.

It was to the church that Jesus said, "'All authority has been given to Me in heaven and on earth. Go therefore and make disciples of all the nations, baptizing them in the name of the Father and of the Son and of the Holy Spirit, teaching them to observe all things that I have commanded you; and lo, I am with you always, even to the end of the age.' Amen" (Matt. 28:18–20).

There have never been more local churches on the face of planet Earth than right now. There's no better investment of a person's time, money, attention, and energy than in the local church. It was designed in the creative genius of Jesus Christ, and it is His ordained channel of redemption in the world.

When the Holy Spirit is living and working in a church, God will bless it and create evergreen opportunities to touch others with the love of Christ. It's hard to invest your life in the work of the Lord if you ignore, neglect, or disdain the church that Jesus established. No, none of them are perfect. Each is filled with people of varying degrees of spiritual maturity, and it's easy to become cynical because of the failures of some of those who attend.

But remember, the churches in the New Testament had problems too. The church in Corinth was an especially painful thorn in the side of the apostle Paul. Yet he told them, "I always thank my God for you because of his grace given you in Christ Jesus. For in him you have been enriched in every way—with all kinds of speech and with all knowledge—God thus confirming our testimony about Christ among you" (1 Cor. 1:4–6 NIV).

Paul wasn't speaking here to an individual but to a group of people—the local, troublesome, imperfect church in Corinth.

If you have a negative attitude toward church, try thanking God for the good people, the good qualities, and the good work of that church. And don't be afraid to invest yourself in it. It is God's chosen instrument to take the gospel to the world.

Invest in God's Wealth

Having invested ourselves in God's Word and God's work, we have to make sure we're investing in God's wealth—in the rich, endless, and lavish future He has laid up for us in heaven.

I said earlier that we're only on earth for a few brief decades, but heaven is our eternal destination. Therefore, we need to make sure we're "paying ahead" and investing our lives in things eternal.

All of us who are in Christ have a great surprise ahead of us. No matter how much we've visualized and anticipated heaven, it'll exceed our expectations by a billion miles and a billion years. Sometimes I read the last two chapters of the Bible, and I try my best to imagine the new heavens and the new earth. I try to envision the city of New Jerusalem and its gold, its glory, and its glitter.

Meditating on things above gives us tremendous comfort, but what a joy to actually see it for ourselves and be heirs of its richness.

The Bible says we can invest in heaven's real estate, as it were. One way we do that is by investing our money in the ongoing progress of the kingdom of God.

The Bible's primary passage about this is in Jesus' Sermon on the Mount, when He said: "Do not lay up for yourselves treasures on earth, where moth and rust destroy and where thieves break in and steal; but lay up for yourselves treasures in heaven, where neither moth nor rust destroys and where thieves do not break in and steal" (Matt. 6:19–20).

In the simplest terms, Jesus said the two ways we invest are in earthly treasures and in heavenly treasures. Earthly treasures are subject to ruin when the moths get them, subject to rust when they corrode, and subject to robbers who break in and steal them. But when you invest in eternal things, it just keeps appreciating out into eternity; you can never give to Him and not receive a hundredfold return—that's a promise.

In fact, Luke 6:38 says when we give, God gives back—but He has a much better way of giving. Notice this: "Give, and it will be given to you: good measure, pressed down, shaken together, and running over will be put into your bosom."

Jesus was talking about the giving that was involved in the gift of grain. He said that when you give to God, God loves to maximize your investment. Randy Alcorn explains:

> Christ offers us the incredible opportunity to trade temporary goods and currency for eternal rewards. By putting our money and possessions in his treasury while we're still on earth, we assure ourselves of eternal rewards beyond comprehension.
>
> Consider the implications of this offer. We can trade temporal possessions we can't keep to gain eternal possessions we can't lose. This is like a child trading bubble gum for a new bicycle, or a man offered ownership of the Coca-Cola company in exchange for a sack of bottle caps. Only a fool would pass up the opportunity.
>
> If we give instead of keep, if we invest in the eternal instead of the temporal, we store up in heaven treasures that will never stop paying dividends.
>
> Whatever treasures we store up in heaven will be waiting for us when we arrive.[10]

Clint Morgan of Nashville recalls watching his parents as he grew up. His mom had the habit of placing her tithe money in a little coin purse every time she got paid. And Clint's dad would quietly drop his tithe in the offering plate every Sunday.

"I saw it and it marked me in a very positive way," Clint wrote. "Our family was far from wealthy. If we weren't poor, we could see it from where we lived. My parents were involved in a church-planting project, and the salary was incredibly small. Dad picked up odd carpentry jobs to provide for us. Mom took on babysitting jobs."

One time the family didn't have enough money for food, but his mom refused to take tithe money from her little coin purse. Later that day, a check came in the mailbox—just enough to buy much-needed groceries!

Looking back on that experience, Clint says, "I walked away from that experience with a solid lesson: whatever has been set aside for God is His; don't use it for any other purpose."[11]

Today it's hard to imagine a safe place to deposit our money. But when we faithfully tithe or devote our resources to the kingdom, it propels the gospel to the world. Souls are saved and heaven is populated. When you support your local church, your funds are transmuted into literature, lives, ministries, and missions. You may never see the returns until you get to heaven, but what a joy it will be to run into folks on the golden streets and learn that it was your gift that helped bring them to faith in Christ.

The Legacy of a Well-Invested Life

I've left the most important thing I have to say for last. As we move forward in this life, we also need to invest in our footprints. In other words, we need to leave a pathway—a legacy of faith—behind us that will lead others to God.

Psalm 71:18 says, "Now also when I am old and grayheaded, O God, do not forsake me, until I declare Your strength to this generation, Your power to everyone who is to come."

William James said, "The great use of a life is to spend it for something that outlasts it."[12] The Bible calls this being rich toward God (Luke 12:21).

I have great admiration for my friend Tony Evans and his powerful ministry. But there would be no ministry without his parents. He said, "My father came to Christ when he was thirty years of age and I was ten. Immediately he became a passionate follower of Christ. My mother didn't like him as a sinner, and she resented him as a saint.

Many times my dad could be found praying and studying the Word in the middle of the night."

About a year after Mr. Evans's conversion, he was studying one night and he heard the steps creak as his wife began making her way from the upstairs bedroom. She saw her husband studying his Bible, but instead of berating him she had tears in her eyes.

Tony recalled, "She told Dad how she had been observing his transformed life over the past year, and that whatever it was that was responsible for it, she wanted it too. That night my father led my mother to Christ. Our home was transformed. After that, Mom and Dad led me, my two brothers, and my sister to Christ."[13]

That evening as he heard the steps creak, Mr. Evans had no idea his simple love for Jesus would transform his home, set his son on the road to ministry, and touch untold thousands of people.

Our days are numbered, and we're moving quickly from today to tomorrow. All our pleasures and possessions are temporary, but the legacy we leave for Christ will endure forever. It's been said many times in many ways, but never better than with these simple words:

THIS ONE LIFE WILL SOON BE PAST,
ONLY WHAT'S DONE FOR CHRIST WILL LAST.

Our love and labor for the Lord is never in vain. Let's not waste a single day. Let's live with eternity in mind! Let's invest in tomorrow and outlive our lives!

Chapter 9

Finish

You're Not Done Until You're Done

If you ever get into an unfortunate scrape, you might hire Frank P. Lucianna to represent you. He's a razor-sharp attorney in Hackensack, New Jersey, just across the Hudson from New York City. You can spot Lucianna in the courtroom daily, dressed in a dapper suit with a pocket square, chopping his hands in the air and defending people in trouble. He does it with energy and effectiveness.

Lucianna has been defending clients for quite a while. Forty-five years ago, a local newspaper claimed he was the city's "busiest criminal lawyer." Twenty-two years ago, the same paper called him "a consummate showman" and New Jersey's "oldest active attorney." Today, Lucianna still waxes eloquent before judges and juries at age ninety-seven.

Lucianna doesn't rest on his laurels. "This is a very consuming profession and it has taken a lot out of my life," he says. "I am constantly involved in preparing cases, and it's a tremendous strain, both mental and physical. Physical because when you go to trial in a case, your whole being is obsessed with trying to help the person you represent, and it places your body and mind under tension."

When asked about his future, Lucianna said, "I hope God lets me continue doing this. I don't want to retire. I don't want to go to Florida. I just want to do what I'm doing."[1]

Personally, I like going to Florida—but otherwise I feel the same. I hope God lets me continue doing what He's called me to do. My name isn't Archippus, but I take the one verse addressed to him in the Bible as though it were written to me: "Tell Archippus: 'See to it that you complete the ministry you have received in the Lord'" (Col. 4:17 NIV).

Yes, your role may change. Your assignments may evolve and your situation may alter. You may have to make adjustments. Even so, one fact won't change: as long as God leaves you on earth, He has ongoing work for you. There's no expiration date to the principles I'm teaching you in this book. You never retire from the Christian life, and you never drop out of God's will.

I urge you—never stop starting, and do your best to finish what you start in the Lord's will.

In his book *Finish: Give Yourself the Gift of Done,* Jon Acuff describes how hard this seems for some people:

> I've only completed 10 percent of the books I own. It took me three years to finish six days of the P90X home exercise program. When I was twenty-three I made it to blue-belt in karate. . . . I have thirty-two half-started Moleskine notebooks in my office and nineteen tubes of nearly finished Chapstick in my bathroom.

Acuff adds that he's not the only one who doesn't stick with things. "According to studies, 92 percent of New Year's resolutions fail. Every January, people start with hope and hype, believing that this will be the New Year that does indeed deliver a New You. But though 100 percent start, only 8 percent finish."[2]

During the 2020 pandemic, I released a book called *Shelter in God* to encourage those struggling with the terrible crisis. One night, as the book was ready to go to press, I awoke with thoughts of all the biblical characters who experienced sheltering-like experiences. The next day, I compiled my list to add it to the epilogue at the end of the book. But then I read a study by Jefferson Smith that said sixty-three percent of readers never finish the book they're reading.[3] I called my publisher at the last possible moment, and we changed the epilogue to a prologue. I didn't want anyone to miss the biblical emphasis of this truth.

It's a little frustrating to think that some people will read the first pages of some of my books and never get to the final pages. I work just as hard on the last page as the first one. But congratulations! You've obviously made it to this point in *Forward*, so don't stop now. Resolve to finish this book. And even more, resolve to finish whatever God places in your hands.

Finish What You Start

Let's face it. You can have a great vision, pray godly prayers, choose the right goals, and focus on the right things. So far, so good. You can also pursue your dreams and make huge investments in God's Word, His work, and His wealth. You can do everything we've talked about so far in this book. But if you don't finish what you start, it's like a building that never has a roof.

Dr. J. Robert Clinton teaches in the School of Intercultural Studies at Fuller Theological Seminary and has devoted vast amounts of time to researching the subject of lifelong leadership development. As part of his study, he identified about a thousand men and women in the Bible who were considered leaders: national leaders, Jewish leaders, church leaders, patriarchs, priests, kings, and so forth.

Many of these leaders were simply mentioned in the text without details, and you may be as surprised as I was to learn there are only forty-nine prominent leaders in Scripture whose lives were surveyed as a whole. We know how they started and how they finished.

Of these forty-nine, only thirty percent finished well. The other seventy percent fell short of God's plan for their lives—a fact that should jolt us. Some leaders such as Samson and Eli stumbled at midlife. Others such as Noah, David, Jehoshaphat, and Hezekiah stumbled near the end.[4]

But thank God for the thirty percent—for people like Joshua, Daniel, Peter, and Paul—who enjoyed walking with God in increasing intimacy throughout their days. They simply kept growing in the grace and knowledge of the Lord. They remained yielded to Him in all things. Like the trees planted in the courtyard of the Lord, they flourished and stayed fresh and green, bearing fruit whatever their age (Ps. 92:12–14).

Clearly, the greatest finisher in the Bible is Jesus. His entire life and ministry was motivated by a commitment to finish the work His Father gave Him to accomplish:

- "Jesus said to them, 'My food is to do the will of Him who sent Me, and to finish His work'" (John 4:34).
- "But I have a greater witness than John's; for the works which the Father has given Me to finish—the very works that I do—bear witness of Me, that the Father has sent Me" (John 5:36).

And when we come to His crucifixion, who can forget perhaps the most profound words in all of the Bible: "So when Jesus had received the sour wine, He said, 'It is finished!'" (John 19:30).

We've explored eight critical steps that move us forward toward God's plan for our lives. In these next few pages I want to have an honest discussion about how to finish well. In some respects I'm preaching to myself. Finishing well has been—and is—one of the most important goals of my life. I've studied this subject through the Bible and read everything I can find.

There are countless barriers to finishing well, but I've discovered five that seem to dominate what I've read on this subject. Rather than present them as barriers, I want to present them as challenges. Let's approach the subject with a positive attitude, because that's fitting for the tone of this book. Consider the remainder of this chapter as a locker-room pep talk delivered to all of us before we head out of the tunnel for the second half of the game.

Stay Focused Till You're Finished

In delivering the halftime pep talk, I would start by reminding you to stay focused. Stay focused until you're finished, until the very last second clicks off the game clock.

One of the great finishers of the Bible was Solomon, King David's son. In fact, the word *finish* is connected with Solomon a dozen times, especially with his building of the temple. I made a list of all the references associated with Solomon completing his assignment to build God's house, and I noticed something that escaped me in all the many times I've read the story.

Solomon was not only a finisher, he was a total, complete, absolute finisher. Notice the inclusion of the word *all* in the phrases used to describe Solomon:

- "He had finished *all* the temple" (1 Kings 6:22).
- "The house was finished in *all* its details and according to *all* its plans" (1 Kings 6:38).
- "So *all* the work that King Solomon had done for the house of the LORD was finished" (1 Kings 7:51).
- "So *all* the work that Solomon had done for the house of the LORD was finished" (2 Chron. 5:1).
- "Solomon successfully accomplished *all* that came into his heart to make in the house of the LORD" (2 Chron. 7:11).

When it came to building God's temple in Jerusalem, Solomon finished it all. He left nothing undone. Perhaps that's because his father, King David, challenged him in 1 Chronicles 28:20: "Be strong and of good courage, and do it; do not fear nor be dismayed, for the LORD God—my God—will be with you. He will not leave you nor forsake you, until you have finished *all the work* for the service of the house of the LORD" (emphasis added).

Most of us underestimate the difficult challenge of finishing. Each year as part of my calling and assignment from God, I write a book. There's a start date and an expected finish date. I take these dates very seriously and try to never miss a deadline. But there's more to the story. Almost all my books have ten chapters; and I research, write, and focus on those chapters until I've completed them. But when I've finished writing the ten chapters, I'm still not finished. There's a dedication page, acknowledgments, a prologue, and often an epilogue. The total manuscript has to be read completely twice: once before it goes to the typesetter and again after it's been typeset.

Over the years, I've learned that I can finish the chapters without too much anxiety, but the remaining items are an emotional challenge. I procrastinate. I dread doing it. It's like pulling teeth to come up with those final words and complete the last details.

Why is that?

I finally figured it out. When I finish the ten chapters, I let myself mentally cross the finish line. I praise the Lord and take my wife out to dinner. The emotional weight of the book is lifted. But in truth the book is not finished, and trying to reengage in the task is a challenge.

The lesson? You're not finished until you're finished. You're not done until you're done. Therefore, stay focused all the way through, because it isn't over until it's over.

When I was in high school, the track coach persuaded me to run the 800-meter race, which, back then, was called the 880-yard race. The strategy I developed then has served me well for life.

First, I tried to go out fast and get a lead. Then, at the beginning of the second lap, I lengthened my stride and tried to hold my lead. As I came around the last curve, I tried to find something deep inside me and run with my whole heart as I focused on the finish line. Without that final kick, I had no chance of winning, and I still remember to this day the feel of my burning lungs and angry leg muscles.

But that's what it takes! Stay focused. Keep your eyes on the goal. Run through the finish tape and then celebrate. The apostle Paul said in his final letter: "I have fought the good fight, I have finished the race, I have kept the faith" (2 Tim. 4:7).

Stay Resilient About Retirement

The second key to finishing well is to approach the topic of retirement with resilience—and with some sanctified resistance. Someone asked the late motivational speaker Zig Ziglar if he was thinking about retiring. He laughed and said, "Retiring? No! I'm re-firing."

My friend Harry Bollback is still active in his midnineties. For the last twenty or so years, people have asked him if he was retired. His reply: "Yes, I retire every night to go to bed so that I can get up the next morning to find out what God has for me to do."

Harry said he wakes up every morning, sits on the edge of his bed, and says, "God, here's another day. I'm glad I'm still here. You must have something for me to do. What I want to do is to magnify Your name. I want to please you in all that I do."[5]

When psychologist Michael Longhurst left his high-level management position in the corporate world, he undertook a major research project on the subject of retirement. He interviewed over two hundred retirees and discovered that too many are unprepared for retirement—especially mentally and emotionally.

One man summed up the problem when he wrote, "I feel so lonely and depressed. I miss my job, the office, my lunch buddies, and friends at work. I used to be very busy at work, and now suddenly there is nothing to do, no deadlines, etc. So, this is what retirement is—boring and lonely. I wish I [could] be happy again like the good old days."[6]

A wife said to her retired husband, "What are you planning to do today?" He replied, "Nothing." She responded, "But you did that yesterday." "I know," he said, "but I'm not finished yet."

Someone said that a husband's retirement can become a wife's full-time job!

Many people have followed the general expectation in America and the western world that when we reach a certain age, we retire. It's just what we do. Retirement has become the final rotation in the cycle of life. Just as we ask children, "What do you want to be when you grow up?" we ask adults, "What do you plan to do when you retire?" Seldom do we hear the value of typical retirement plans questioned, and certainly not the value of retirement itself.

But retirement as we know it today was virtually nonexistent throughout history. Retirement made little sense when the average life expectancy was only thirty or forty years. It has its roots in the early 1900s, when many large American industries, including railroads, banks, and oil companies, began offering pensions.

In 1935, President Franklin D. Roosevelt introduced the Social Security Act. An employee's income was taxed throughout his or her working life to fund a retirement income beginning at age sixty-five. In America today, most workers expect to retire, and the culture is geared to accommodate it.

Interestingly, the Bible records only one example of retirement: "This is what pertains to the Levites: From twenty-five years old and above one may enter to perform service in the work of the tabernacle of meeting; and at the age of fifty years they must cease performing this work, and shall work no more. They may minister with their brethren in the tabernacle of meeting, to attend to needs, but they themselves shall do no work" (Num. 8:24–26).

While the Levite tabernacle workers were instructed to retire at age fifty, they were not put out to pasture to spend the rest of their lives twiddling their thumbs and gazing at the sundial. They were charged to minister to the younger Levites who took over their jobs. They became mentors and advisors. Today they would probably hand out cards calling themselves consultants.

I'm not saying you shouldn't take advantage of your Social Security income or pension benefits. But you might want to avoid the word *retirement*. You don't have to continue in your profession until you're in your nineties, like our lawyer friend Frank Lucianna. But if you do leave your job, remember—retirement is simply God's way of freeing you up for further service.

Stay Connected to Your Calling

After staying focused and continuing to do God's work, I implore you to stay connected to your calling from God. While some experts extol the virtues of wholesale change after retirement, I've observed that those who finish best never consider themselves retired from their basic calling from God. There is no "best if used before" stamped onto your soul. The Bible says, "The gifts and the calling of God are irrevocable" (Rom. 11:29).

Os Guinness had something to say about this:

> I think it's important to recognize that we can retire from our jobs, but we can never retire from our calling. Calling gives us our sense of task or responsibility, right up to the last day we spend on earth, when we will go to meet the Caller. I think that gives life incredible value, and therefore the prosperity of finishing well is that we continue to have a sense of responsibility and engagement that makes each day we live enormously important. This is also a subject in which the Christian view provides such a compelling contrast with the secular view, which tells you that you're over the hill when you reach a certain age.[7]

To finish well, consider maintaining a connection between what you did before you retired and what you do afterward. Someone said, "Your career is what you are paid to do. Your calling is what you were made to do."

One of the most influential people in my life was Howard Hendricks, one of my professors at Dallas Theological Seminary. My wife, Donna, was his secretary while I was a student. He was an incredible teacher and a master motivator. When Bob Buford interviewed him for his book *Finishing Well*, Dr. Hendricks said: "The average person dies between two and seven years after retirement, and it's simply because they've lost their purpose in life. For most of them, their purpose was wrapped up in their work, and once they're no longer working they feel they have no meaning in their lives. They retire *from* something rather than *to* something."

Hendricks went on to apply this principle to himself: "I've done a lot of things in my life," he said, "but only one thing gives me ultimate satisfaction, and that's teaching. If I stop teaching I lose the reason for which I was put on the planet . . . this is what I was born to do. . . . If the Seminary decides it's time for me to move on, I'll just go teach in another venue. . . . I'll spend the rest of my life teaching."[8]

Many of my friends who pastored all their lives and then retired have just kept on doing what they've always done. They fill pulpits on the weekends. They become interim pastors in churches waiting for full-time pastors. They find new ways and means of teaching and preaching. And many of them relish the change. They're able to keep doing what they love without all the administrative hassles present in most churches today.

I have a good friend who loves to preach but hates administration. When I heard he'd resigned from his church, I called to ask about it. He took my call, but instead of saying "Hello," he exclaimed, "Free at last. Free at last. Thank God Almighty, I am free at last."

He meant he was free now to do what he really loved without the distractions of what he didn't enjoy.

You may not have a career that's transferable into your post-retirement life, but if you're a follower of Christ, you have a calling. You have a gift. God has given you an ability for service. So just keep using it for the Lord.

My father, Dr. James T. Jeremiah, devoted most of his adult life to Cedarville College, a small Baptist college near Dayton, Ohio. He was the president of that college for twenty-five years and the chancellor for another twenty-five years. My father retired at age sixty-two, but he was not finished serving. Every week he was still out preaching in churches and speaking at banquets, representing the college. His itinerary took him to places where graduates of Cedarville were in places of leadership such as pastoring, leading, and administrating.

One day my father was asked, "Dr. Jeremiah, what have you been doing since you retired from the presidency?" My dad said, "I have been clipping coupons from a lifetime of investment." I never forgot those words. I suggest to you that there's no better way to fulfill your calling than that!

When Jesus had finished his work on earth and was about to be crucified, resurrected, and returned to heaven, He prayed this summary statement about His life: "I have glorified You on the earth. I have finished the work which You have given Me to do" (John 17:4).

Read that verse again carefully and you'll notice that Jesus did not finish all the work there was to do. He finished all the work that *He was given to do*. That is what our prayer should be. "Lord, help me to finish the work You have given me to do." If you do that you'll have a full and exciting life.

Stay Vigilant After Your Victories

Finishing well also demands vigilance. We can't let down our guard, especially after new adventures or fresh victories.

In 2012, Donna and I visited Switzerland for the first time. We ended our tour in Zermatt, the beautiful village that lies at the base of the Matterhorn. The north face of this mountain, called Hornli Ridge, is an almost straight-up climb; it was hard to imagine anyone making it to the summit. But many climbers have navigated their way to the top of Hornli Ridge.

At the foot of the Matterhorn there's a cemetery called Mountaineer's Cemetery. Most of the people buried there are casualties of the Matterhorn. But here was my strange finding: many who died on this mountain died while descending after having reached the top.

Here is what was written on one gravestone:

IN MEMORY OF
DAVID ROBINSON
OF WAKEFIELD AND
BANGOR NORTH WALES
WHOSE UNTIMELY DEATH
AT THE AGE OF 24 YEARS
OCCURED WHILE DESCENDING
THE HORNLI RIDGE
HAVING CLIMBED THE
NORTH FACE OF THE
MATTERHORN ON
DECEMBER 28, 1976

What a lesson this was for me and should be for all of us: we are the most vulnerable to failure after we achieve our greatest success.

During World War II, England's Royal Air Force psychologists discovered that pilots made the most errors as they flew their planes back in for a landing, returning to their bases after flying successful missions. "The cause was an almost irresistible tendency to relax."[9]

Like pilots and mountain climbers, we can become enamored of our achievements and fail to focus on finishing what we started.

I think that's what got King David into trouble with Bathsheba. He'd achieved great success, winning every battle against his enemies and creating great peace in Israel. But David got careless: "It happened in the spring of the year, at the time when kings go out to battle, that David sent Joab and his servants with him, and all Israel. . . . But David remained at Jerusalem" (2 Sam. 11:1).

King David should have been leading his people and serving at the head of his army, but instead he stayed home. He felt he was at the point in life when he could relax some and let others bear the burden of war. He wasn't where he should have been, and he wasn't doing what he should have been doing!

David was celebrating his victories without vigilance, and the rest is history. His sin with Bathsheba and the murder of her husband, Uriah, is a black stain on David's life. And while God forgave David and restored him, that one moment of carelessness—that lack of vigilance—became part of David's biography.

The Bible says, "David did what was right in the eyes of the LORD, and had not turned aside from anything that He commanded him all the days of his life, *except in the matter of Uriah the Hittite*" (1 Kings 15:5, emphasis added).

Elijah had a similar experience. He stood alone on Mount Carmel and called down fire from God upon the prophets of Baal. He personally witnessed the terrible might and power of the Lord. But then, Queen Jezebel threatened to have him killed, and he ran for his life, begging God to kill him: "He arose and ran for his life . . . and he prayed that he might die, and said, 'It is enough! Now, LORD, take my life'" (1 Kings 19:3–4).

I believe there are two verses in the Bible we should all memorize and keep before us. They tell us what to do in order not to fall and they capture this vigilance-after-victory warning:

- "Pride goes before destruction, and a haughty spirit before a fall" (Prov. 16:18).
- "Therefore let him who thinks he stands take heed lest he fall" (1 Cor. 10:12).

Stay Ready for Redeployment

And now, the fifth and final key to finishing well: don't finish at all! Always be looking forward to what the Lord has for you next.

It doesn't take a deep dive into secular history or the Bible to discover that many great things are accomplished by people past the age of retirement.

Pianist-comedian Victor Borge, "the Clown Prince of Denmark," continued to delight huge audiences until his death at age ninety-one. As I write this, singer Tony Bennett is ninety-three and leaves his heart not only in San Francisco but also in many other cities where he continues to perform.

At ninety years old master cellist Pablo Casals was asked why he kept practicing eight hours a day. He replied, "I think I'm improving."

The apostle Paul was over sixty when he made his grueling voyage to Rome, where he preached, wrote, and taught until his execution four years later. He had no intention of slowing down, much less retiring to rest on his laurels. At his miraculous conversion thirty years earlier, Paul had found his life's passion. He was doing exactly what he was called to do, what he loved to do, and it absorbed him completely.

Right now, I'm fourteen years past normal retirement age (and please don't do the math!). The other day I began thinking about some of the incredible things I've been allowed by God to do since I didn't retire.

- I preached in one of the largest churches in the world. Calvary Temple in Hyderabad, India, holds five services each Sunday starting at 5:30 in the morning. I preached in all five services to well over one hundred thousand people. On the Monday after this amazing Sunday, I preached the ordination service for the son of the church's founder and pastor, Pastor Satish Kumar. I still can't believe I was privileged to do this. I will always be so thankful for this opportunity.

- I released the *Jeremiah Study Bible,* which is now available in the New King James, the New International, and the English Standard versions.
- At the church where I pastor, we built a $30 million Generations building that has revolutionized how we go about our ministries.
- I saw our Turning Point radio network grow to three thousand radio stations across the United States.
- I wrote and released fourteen new books.
- I fulfilled a long-term dream and led one thousand people on a tour of Israel, where I taught the Bible on the very sites where the events occurred.
- I visited the beautiful country of Switzerland twice.
- I had a part in producing three Christmas specials in New York City that were seen during the Christmas season by millions of people.

What I've just written could be mistaken for a bragging list, but it most certainly is not. It is a gratitude list, for these are the things God has allowed me to do after most of the world says I should have retired. And on top of that I would add all the truths I've discovered and rediscovered in Scripture.

Pearl Buck, the famous writer and the daughter of missionaries to China, said: "I have reached an honorable position in life because I am old and no longer young. I am a far more useful person than I was fifty years ago, or forty years ago, or thirty, twenty, or even ten. I have learned so much since I was seventy."[10]

So don't give up on yourself too early. Don't deprive yourself of the many blessings God wants to bestow upon you in your post-retirement years. Change what you do if you must, but don't stop serving the Lord.

Nine times in the Bible (ESV) we find the words *old and advanced in years*. I've always thought this phrase was an illustration of unnecessary redundancy. If you say someone is old, you shouldn't have to add the words *advanced in years*. That seems like piling on.

But every word in the Bible is important, and one day I noticed something fascinating. Many of the times when that redundant phrase appears in the Bible, it's a description of a person who is about to experience something astounding. For example:

- Abraham (one hundred years old) and Sarah (age ninety) were "old, well advanced in age" as they are about to become the parents of Isaac (Gen. 18:11).
- Zacharias and Elizabeth were "old and advanced in years" before they gave birth to John the Baptist (Luke 1:18).
- Joshua is also described this way before he received his marching orders to enter the land of God's promise: "Now Joshua was old, advanced in years. And the LORD said to him: 'You are old, advanced in years, and there remains very much land yet to be possessed'" (Josh. 13:1).

Here are some verses to encourage you to keep on keeping on. They were given to us by our gracious God to keep us faithful throughout our lives. Don't forget what we learned earlier: "If you're not dead, you're not done!"

- "The righteous shall flourish like a palm tree, he shall grow like a cedar in Lebanon. Those who are planted in the house of the LORD shall flourish in the courts of our God. They shall still bear fruit in old age; they shall be fresh and flourishing" (Ps. 92:12–14).
- "Even to your old age, I am He, and even to gray hairs I will carry you! I have made, and I will bear; even I will carry, and will deliver you" (Isa. 46:4).

And here is the special prayer I have claimed for my life: "Now also when I am old and grayheaded, O God, do not forsake me, until I declare Your strength to this generation, Your power to everyone who is to come" (Ps. 71:18).

Finish Well

As we bring this chapter on finishing to a close, I want to tell you about one of the laymen in our congregation. More than anyone I know, he has captured the concept of finishing well.

Tom Heyer taught math at Helix High School for forty years. He had received Christ as Savior as a junior at San Diego State University and immediately began to teach. He loved his job! I remember meeting him at his school many years ago and could tell he was not just putting in time. He loved his students. He also helped start a Christian club on campus that impacted many lives.

In the summer of 2002, Tom Heyer was looking forward to beginning his fortieth year of teaching. One morning as he and his wife, Pam, took their regular prayer walk together, God spoke to Tom and turned his life upside down. Here is how Tom put it: "That morning God spoke directly to me. He told me it was time to set aside teaching because He had something else for me to do."

Since teaching had been his whole life, Tom had no idea what God was up to, but he was about to find out. After counseling with one of our pastors, Tom accepted the challenge to start a weekly men's Bible study. The Bible study named itself "Fellows" and has been going on for eighteen years.

Because of his leadership in that Bible study, Tom was asked if he'd be willing to take over the prison ministry at our church, Shadow Mountain Community Church. At that time about twelve people were involved in ministering to the prisoners of San Diego County.

Tom accepted the challenge, and what has happened since is truly remarkable. Today as he closes in on the seventeenth year in this ministry, God has opened doors for ministry to everyone impacted by incarceration: inmates, parolees, ex-offenders, spouses, children, other family members—even correctional officers and prison staff. According to Tom, the "p" in prison does not stand for "prison" but for "people"—people whom God loves with an everlasting, unconditional love.

Each week, forty different Shadow Mountain team members go into eight different prisons, holding roughly thirty meetings a month, with an average of over six hundred inmates (men, women, and youth) in attendance.

At Christmas, a huge party is hosted for the children of incarcerated parents. Hundreds of children, mostly with their mothers, attend this party on our church campus. On the Saturday before Christmas our event center is filled with families that would be forgotten were it not for this incredible ministry.

Several years ago, a young man in our church who'd been incarcerated was released. He came to Tom and shared how Christmas is the lowest time of the year for prisoners. He wondered if there was anything we could do to make a difference in their lives during this season.

The result of that conversation was "The Great Christmas Card Mail Out." Last Christmas, hundreds of volunteers in San Diego, under the direction of Tom Heyer's Shadow Mountain Prison Ministry, sent out over fifteen thousand Christmas cards to inmates.

When God spoke to Tom Heyer on that morning walk in 2002, he ignited a movement that will live on long after both Tom and I are gone. Today, the Shadow Mountain Prison Ministry is one of the largest church-sponsored prison ministries in America. And it all started in the life of one man who had just retired. Tom Heyer was ready to be redeployed.

Are you?

Chapter 10
Celebrate

Turn Your Forward into Forever

You might say Luke Pittard relished his job at a McDonald's in Cardiff, Wales. But he walked away from it after winning the UK National Lottery. After all, he was an overnight millionaire.

Luke celebrated his good fortune by marrying his girlfriend, Emma, also a McDonald's employee. They bought a house and took a long holiday in the Canary Islands. But after returning to Wales, Luke was bored. "To be honest," he said, "there's only so much relaxing you can do. I'm . . . young, and a bit of hard work never did anyone any harm."

Luke asked for his old job back, and now you can find him flipping hamburgers again at McDonald's. He makes more money from the interest on his winnings than at the restaurant, but he feels a natural need to work and to be with his friends and coworkers. "They all think I'm a bit mad but I tell them there's more to life than money," he says.

Emma added, "I can totally understand it. We both really enjoyed working at McDonald's and still have good friends there. So it was very familiar for him and something for him to look forward to."[1]

We all need a break now and then, but we don't need an endless holiday. Instead, what we need is meaningful work, close friends, and something to look forward to. Those facts will never change, not in this life and not in heaven!

When you have a relationship with God through Jesus Christ, you're wealthier than the winner of the richest lottery. Remember—much of our treasure is ahead of us in heaven. But many people are afraid they'll be bored there. It's remarkable how many people—even Christians—harbor mixed feelings along these lines. They ask: "What if I get to heaven and I'm bored? After all, there's only so much relaxing I can do. What if I miss my friends? What if I long for the kind of activity that enriched my life on earth?"

Don't worry, God is not boring!

Heaven won't bore you; it will bring fulfillment and celebration! All your dreaming, praying, focusing, risk-taking, and investing—all your forward momentum on earth—is a prelude to greater service, happier work, and richer fulfillment in your heavenly home. God's children are always moving forward, even as they depart earth.

Look Forward to Heaven

The heroes of Scripture thought of heaven constantly, confessing they were strangers and pilgrims on the earth, seeking a homeland, desiring a better country—a heavenly one—and looking forward to the city with foundations "whose builder and maker is God" (Heb. 11:10). Jesus, too, longed for heaven as He approached the end of His earthly life, telling His disciples, "If you loved Me, you would rejoice because I said, 'I am going to the Father'" (John 14:28).

The apostle Peter said something important about this. Notice the words in italics, for they reveal the attitude we should have about heaven:

> You ought to live holy and godly lives as you *look forward* to the day of God and speed its coming. That day will bring about the destruction of the heavens by fire, and the elements will melt in the heat. But in keeping with his promise we are *looking forward* to a new heaven and a new earth, where righteousness dwells. So then, dear friends, since you are *looking forward* to this, make every effort to be found spotless, blameless and at peace with him. (2 Pet. 3:11–14 NIV)

Three times Peter told us to look forward, to anticipate what God has for us in the future: the return of Christ, the creation of the new heaven and the new earth, and our eternal home in heaven. Our anticipation empowers us to live holy, godly, and purposeful lives in this present age.

Ange Shepard grew up in a small town in scenic Nova Scotia. At age ten, she became enthralled with Southern California, particularly Los Angeles. She watched television shows filmed there and was fascinated by the big city, the celebrity lifestyle, the glitter, the palm trees, the incredible weather.

Ange learned that 323 was one of the area codes for the Los Angeles area, and she would get on the phone and dial 1–323 and then seven random numbers. Sometimes the call would be answered, and Ange would say, "Hi, is this LA?" When the person said, "Yes," Ange would hang up, thrilled to have talked to someone in Los Angeles.

Her calls came to an end when her dad saw the phone bill—but her daydreams did not. Ange always imagined that one day she'd live in LA. "I didn't know when or how I was going to get there," she recalls. "I just knew for certain I was going to leave my small town and live out my dreams in Los Angeles."

She was twenty-four when she visited California for the first time—with a one-way ticket. Today Ange still calls LA home. She's living her dream.[2]

I live in Southern California and love it, too, though believe me, it has its problems. But Ange's story interests me because she longed for a city. That city occupied her mind day and night, and its glittering allure drove her dreams and guided her life. She even called to talk to random people simply because they lived in the LA area code.

I long for a place better than Southern California and for a city greater than Los Angeles, don't you? Anticipating the heavenly city of God should be the driving force of our lives, especially because through prayer we can stay in constant communication with Someone who already lives there.

The Bible says, "Seek those things which are above, where Christ is, sitting at the right hand of God" (Col. 3:1).

Will that make us too "heavenly minded"? Listen to what C. S. Lewis said about that:

A continual looking forward to the eternal world is not (as some modern people think) a form of escapism or wishful thinking, but one of the things a Christian is meant to do. It does not mean that we are to leave the present world as it is. If you read history you will find that the Christians who did most for the present world were just those who thought most of the next.

He continued,

The Apostles themselves, who set on foot the conversion of the Roman Empire, the great men who built up the Middle Ages, the English Evangelicals who abolished the Slave Trade, all left their mark on Earth, precisely because their minds were occupied with Heaven. It is since Christians have largely ceased to think of the other world that they have become so ineffective in this. Aim at heaven and you will get Earth "thrown in": aim at Earth and you will get neither.[3]

What, then, can you and I expect in heaven? What kind of celebrations will we discover in God's eternal home?

Look Forward to a Rousing Welcome

First, expect a rousing welcome. Most of us are apprehensive about dying. Like the ancient Israelites crossing the Jordan, we "have not passed this way before" (Josh. 3:4). But the Bible is full of information to alleviate your concern. The apostle Peter said that if you serve the Lord Jesus faithfully, "you will receive a rich welcome into the eternal kingdom of our Lord and Savior Jesus Christ" (2 Pet. 1:11 NIV).

A rich welcome!

It's easy to underestimate these words. Recently a little boy in Ohio named Grady went back to school after having been diagnosed with leukemia. He'd missed a year with his classmates because of his treatments, but finally he was able to return for a few hours a day. On his first day back, the principal met him and opened the door. In front of Grady were all the students and teachers lining the hall holding strands of bright crepe paper. They yelled and cheered as eight-year-old Grady ran between them. At the end of the hall a giant sign said, "Welcome back, Grady!" The children clapped and laughed, and teachers wiped tears from their eyes. Arriving home later that day, Grady said, "This was the best day ever mom! I had so much fun. . . . I didn't know days could be this good!"[4]

If school children could pull off a welcome celebration like that, think of what Almighty God and His angels can do! You are promised a "rich welcome" into heaven. It'll be your best day ever. You can't imagine that a day could be so good.

Your "rich welcome" actually begins before you arrive in heaven. In our Lord's parable of the rich man and the beggar Lazarus, we're told, "The time came when the beggar died and the angels carried him to Abraham's side" in heaven (Luke 16:22 NIV). I believe the Lord sends an angelic escort to accompany His departing saints to heaven. You'll not be forgotten, forsaken, or alone for a single second. And you'll arrive there to find you are Home at last!

Singer Michael Bublé loved his grandfather, Don Demetrio Santaga, who built a house in Vancouver fifty years ago and lived in it until his dying day. Santaga loved his house and hoped it would stay in the family after his death. During the final eight years of his life, Santaga was unable to live alone, so Bublé hired a Filipina healthcare worker named Minette to care for him.

At first Santaga resented having a nurse, but the two quickly became close. Bublé and Santaga came to view Minette as part of the family, and near the end of his life, Santaga shared his final wish with his grandson.

When the older man died, Minette took the opportunity to return to the Philippines to visit her family, whom she had been supporting with her income. While she was gone, Jonathan and Drew Scott, the celebrity "Property Brothers," came to Vancouver and did extensive renovations on Santaga's home. It was an amazing makeover.

When Minette returned, she was met with television cameras from the crew of *Celebrity IOU*. Michael opened the door and ushered her in, saying, "Welcome home." Minette's hands flew to her mouth and her eyes filled with tears. "It is so much, really so much," she said. "I have no words right now. It hasn't sunk in yet. It's beautiful."

"You can only imagine what it's going to mean to her," said Bublé.[5]

If you want to imagine how you'll feel when you see your amazing new Home, listen to what the martyr Stephen said in the New Testament. As he died, he looked up to heaven and saw the glory of God and Jesus standing at the right hand of God. He shouted, "Look! I see the heavens opened and the Son of Man standing at the right hand of God!" (Acts 7:56).

As the first person to give his life for Christ, Stephen's experience is unique. But to some extent it surely anticipates the "rich welcome" you'll receive the moment you're transported to heaven and Jesus says to you, "Enter into the joy of your lord" (Matt. 25:21).

Look Forward to a Rich Reward

Among the joys of heaven will be the rewards given for faithfulness on earth. If you live according to biblical principles (such as the ones I've articulated in this book), there's a series of rewards for you described in the Bible. Jesus often said things like:

- "Whoever gives one of these little ones only a cup of cold water in the name of a disciple, assuredly, I say to you, he shall by no means lose his reward" (Matt. 10:42).
- "Rejoice in that day and leap for joy! For indeed your reward is great in heaven" (Luke 6:23).
- "But love your enemies, do good, and lend, hoping for nothing in return; and your reward will be great" (Luke 6:35).

The apostle Paul picked up the theme, saying, "And whatever you do, do it heartily, as to the Lord and not to men, knowing that from the Lord you will receive the reward of the inheritance" (Col. 3:23–24).

Hebrews 11:6 says God is "a rewarder of those who diligently seek Him."

Did you know that at fabulous awards shows like the Oscars, even those who lose still get gifts? According to *Forbes* magazine, every Oscar nominee gets a gift bag valued (in 2020) at $225,000.

What could be in a gift bag worth nearly a quarter of a million dollars? The items range from a box of cookies to a certificate for plastic surgery. There might be some Hotsy Totsy Haus amethyst bath bombs, valued at $75 each. You might find a voucher good for a twelve-day cruise on a yacht with butler service, a helicopter, and a spa. Some bags contain a trip on a submarine, and others a gift card redeemable for a romantic getaway at a Spanish lighthouse converted into a luxury hotel. You'll also find $25,000 worth of cosmetics and rejuvenation procedures in the bag, along with a two-pack of dark chocolate Milanos.

How much greater is the "abundance of grace and of the gift of righteousness" that the Lord offers us (Rom. 5:17)! For the genuine follower of Christ, one word of welcome or commendation by our Lord is a million times better than Oscar's gift bag.

Joni Eareckson Tada wrote, "If God hadn't told us differently, we'd all think this parade of life would go on forever. But it will end. This life is not forever, nor is it the best life that will ever be. The fact is that believers are headed for heaven. It is reality. And what we do here on Earth has a direct bearing on how we will live there."[6]

We're often too concerned about the petty awards of earth and not sufficiently concerned about the rich rewards waiting for us in heaven.

The Bible teaches there will be a moment in the future when our work for the Lord will be evaluated. This is called the judgment seat of Christ (2 Cor. 5:10). I believe it will occur immediately after the rapture of the church to heaven. This has nothing to do with our eternal destination, for all those in Christ Jesus are heaven-bound by grace. As I wrote in *The Book of Signs*, "This judgment is for Christ to assess every believer's earthly works to determine what rewards are to be received."[7]

The Bible often describes these rewards as "crowns."

There is the *Victor's Crown*, described in 1 Corinthians 9:24–25: "Run in such a way that you may obtain [this crown]. And everyone who competes for the prize is temperate in all things. Now they do it to obtain a perishable crown, but we for an imperishable crown." This is God's reward for those Christians who live a disciplined, godly life on earth.

There is the *Crown of Rejoicing*, which Paul described in 1 Thessalonians 2:19, when he told Christians in the city of Thessalonica, "For what is our hope, or joy, or crown of rejoicing? Is it not even you in the presence of our Lord Jesus Christ at His coming?" This is the joy of seeing those in heaven who were influenced for Christ by our lives, deeds, and words.

There is the *Crown of Righteousness*. The key to this reward is developing an intense desire for the Lord's return. The apostle Paul said, "Finally, there is laid up for me the crown of righteousness, which the Lord, the righteous Judge, will give to me on that Day, and not to me only but also to all who have loved His appearing" (2 Tim. 4:8).

Next, the *Crown of Life*, given for those who endure temptations and trials: "Blessed is the man who endures temptation; for when he has been approved, he will receive the crown of life which the Lord has promised to those who love Him" (James 1:12).

Finally, there is the *Crown of Glory*, which Peter described like this: "When the Chief Shepherd appears, you will receive the crown of glory that does not fade away" (1 Pet. 5:4).

Robert Webb of New Zealand was surprised recently when he became the recipient of the Queen's Birthday Honours. These are special awards given on Queen Elizabeth's birthday to people who have been faithful volunteers in local communities across the United Kingdom. Webb's award was for his care of birds.

It started years ago during Webb's regular trips to Auckland as a truck driver. He often saw injured birds beside the road. He began stopping, picking them up, and caring for them until they were ready to return to their native habitats. Sometimes Webb would be caring for thirty birds at once. Over time, he became known as the person to see if you found an injured bird.

Eventually, Webb's efforts led to the establishment of the Native Bird Recovery Centre, which today includes a surgical unit, incubation room for hatching kiwi eggs, recovery pens, and a bird hospital. There are also three aviaries for birds too badly injured to be released into the wild. Webb takes some of the more spectacular birds into classrooms to teach schoolchildren about conservation.

When Webb was given the award, a reporter asked him if he was planning to retire. He replied, "We get too much enjoyment from the birds to retire. Seeing a bird come into the center, making it safe and then seeing it fly again—you feel you've achieved something in life, and that's the biggest reward."[8]

Jesus, too, was concerned about the sparrows of the air. And Webb's words convey how you'll feel about the rewards God gives you. The greatest reward will be seeing those in heaven who've been influenced by your work. That's when you'll understand you've achieved something in life after all—far more than you realized, for your labor in the Lord is never in vain (1 Cor. 15:58).

Look Forward to a Resurrected Body

It's also important to remember we aren't going to be ghosts, angels, or disembodied spirits in heaven. At the moment of our rapture or resurrection, we're also going to celebrate our new, glorified bodies. We're not going to be like Lazarus, who was raised from death in John 11. He hobbled out in his grave clothes, and others cut him out of the shroud. No, we'll be like Jesus, whose resurrected body passed right through His grave clothes.

Lazarus rose to die again; Jesus rose never again to age, experience illness, face weakness, or encounter death. Philippians 3 says the Lord Jesus "will transform our lowly bodies so that they will be like his glorious body" (v. 21 NIV).

This is very good news! Some of those reading this book are battling illnesses, disabilities, and the ravages of aging. Medical science is grappling with all those issues, and some of our advances are amazing.

Sergeant John Peck is an American marine who lost all four limbs to an explosion in Afghanistan in 2010. At first, he thought he'd spend the rest of his life wearing prosthetic arms and legs. But—I can hardly believe this—in 2016 he received a double-arm transplant. The limbs came from a young man who was declared brain dead and whose arms were rushed in ice packs to an operating room in Boston for the fourteen-hour transplant surgery, performed by a team of sixty surgeons, nurses, and technicians. When Peck woke up the next day, he had someone else's arms.[9]

Today John Peck is able to perform many daily tasks with his new arms, including signing copies of his book, *Rebuilding Sergeant Peck*.

If human medical technology can do so much to help our bodies recover from horrific tragedies, imagine what God can do instantaneously at the moment of resurrection: "We will all be changed—in a flash, in the twinkling of an eye, at the last trumpet. For the trumpet will sound, the dead will be raised imperishable, and we will be changed" (1 Cor. 15:51–52 NIV).

Consider what we know about the resurrection body of Christ. It was His own natural body, recognizable, with His unique DNA, His personal essence and qualities. It was the same body He acquired, in embryonic form, at conception. But in a flash of Easter glory it was transformed into an imperishable body, with new capabilities and new incapabilities.

Jesus' resurrected body was incapable of aging, illness, and death. But it was capable of passing through doors, ascending into the air, eating food, and touching His friends. His resurrection body is the pattern for our own.

Look Forward to a Renewed Assignment

You'll need your resurrection body because you have a lot of work ahead of you. One of the greatest aspects of heaven involves the prospect of more service! I'm like the hamburger flipper at the beginning of this chapter: I have little interest in sitting and relaxing for eons on end. You need some refreshing rest but not aimless monotony.

Twice in the book of Revelation we're told we'll be involved in meaningful tasks and acts of service in heaven.

Revelation 7:15 says, "Therefore they are before the throne of God, and serve Him day and night." And Revelation 22:3 says, "And there shall be no more curse, but the throne of God and of the Lamb shall be in it, and His servants shall serve Him."

Randy Alcorn wrote extensively about this in his book on heaven, saying, "Work in Heaven won't be frustrating or fruitless; instead, it will involve lasting accomplishment, unhindered by decay and fatigue, enhanced by unlimited resources. We'll approach our work with the enthusiasm we bring to our favorite sport or hobby."

He continues, "In Heaven, we'll reign with Christ, exercise leadership and authority, and make important decisions. This implies we'll be given specific responsibilities by our leaders and we'll delegate specific responsibilities to those under our leadership (Luke 19:17–19). We'll set goals, devise plans, and share ideas. Our best work days on the present Earth . . . are just a small foretaste of the joy our work will bring us on the New Earth."[10]

Perhaps our occupations in heaven will be an extension of our work on earth or of those duties that brought us the most joy. Of course, some occupations won't exist in heaven. There will be no physicians because there will be no illness. Police officers won't be needed, nor prison guards. There won't even be evangelists, for everyone will know Christ.

But there will be musicians! There may also be teachers, for we won't be omniscient. We'll be capable of learning and teaching what we learn. We know there will be layers of authority and responsibility in the administration of the new heavens and the new earth (Luke 19:17). I expect some of us will be scientists because God's new heavens and new earth will be full of surprises to investigate.

You'll have plenty of time to undertake new vocations, hobbies, and pursuits. With eternity to practice, you'll be able to master great symphonies, create wonderful works of art, play extreme sports, write books, deliver lectures, explore exotic locations, and enjoy thrills without risk. All along the way, there will be meaningful work and fulfilling activities.

When God placed Adam and Eve in the garden of Eden, He didn't expect them to sit around frolicking and feasting all the time. He told them to tend the garden (Gen. 2:15). When we see Adam and Eve on the new earth, I wouldn't be surprised to find them about their original tasks—tending to the gardens that line the Crystal River and enclose the Tree of Life (Rev. 22:1–2).

When Jesus ascended and returned to heaven, He didn't retire from His work. He resumed His place on the throne, sustaining the universe (Col. 1:17) and building and directing the work of His earthly church. He is interceding for us (Rom. 8:34) and preparing a place for us (John 14:3). He said, "My Father is always working, and so am I" (John 5:17 NLT).

If Jesus is busy in heaven, how wonderful to share in His work! Think of the most fulfilling thing you've done on earth—then consider the fact that in heaven, even the smallest action will surpass the joy of that earthly moment. Your work on earth, whatever God is assigning you right now, is preparatory to eternal service in heaven. That's something worth celebrating.

Look Forward to a Royal Throne

By far the greatest energy and enthusiasm in heaven will be around the throne of God when we cast our crowns at His feet and worship Him with full understanding and joy. We have a preview in Revelation 4 and 5, when the saints and angels of heaven sing in a loud voice, "Blessing and honor and glory and power be to Him who sits on the throne, and to the Lamb, forever and ever!" (Rev. 5:13).

Dr. Vernon Whaley has been training worship leaders for decades. His passion for worship stems from the small Alaska church he attended as a child. His parents were missionaries there, and they had a deep concern for people with disabilities. When they met for the services, it was a remarkable crowd—an alcoholic turned deacon; a prostitute transformed into a Sunday School teacher; a blind man who played the piano; a former fugitive who kept the church grounds; a young woman lame from birth; a young man with Down syndrome who helped take the offering. But they all sang praises to God.

"My father was a great one for having extended times of singing during the Sunday night services," recalls Dr. Whaley. "My father entered the ministry during the 1940s when giant Youth for Christ rallies were held all over the country. He never lost the excitement of those rallies and their impact on his life. So on almost every Sunday night, our congregation resounded with [hymn after hymn]."

Dr. Whaley recalls one Sunday night when there was a puzzling stir from the middle of the congregation. He turned around to see a significantly disabled girl slowly steering her wheelchair to the front of the church. The converted alcoholic got up and helped her roll to the front of the pulpit. Rev. Whaley came down near her. Using her alphabet slate, she told him she wanted to sing a solo. She wanted to sing "Amazing Grace."

The blind pianist struck up the tune for "Amazing Grace," and the girl began making groans and moanings in time with the music. "I was not able to clearly understand a word she sang," Dr. Whaley recalls. "But somehow the musicianship and articulation of words did not matter. All of us understood intuitively what she was doing and more important—why she was doing it. There was no doubt. We all knew she was singing from her heart to the living God. There was not a dry eye in the audience. Even the children were captured and stilled by the moment."[11]

Can you image the moment tens of millions of us join the tens of millions of angels—all our disabilities gone, all our problems solved, all our burdens lifted—and we lift our voices in a choir of billions and sing of God's amazing grace!

The prophet Isaiah said, "Your eyes will see the King in His beauty" (Isa. 33:17). Think of the most exciting arena you've ever been in—a great church service, evangelistic rally, ball game, or musical concert. Then magnify the excitement by a million times, and you may get a glimpse of the celebration you'll feel as you join your voice, singing: "Alleluia! For the Lord God Omnipotent reigns! Let us be glad and rejoice and give Him glory!" (Rev. 19:6–7).

Look Forward to a Rapturous Reunion

Here's something else. As you gather around the throne, you'll look over and see your dearest loved ones in Christ. You'll instantly know each other, and you'll begin fellowshipping in heaven where you left off on earth. All the saints of all the ages will be there, plus all the angels. No more separation! No more sorrow! I'll see my dad and mom again, and my dearest ones who have preceded me to glory.

The Australian press recently reported on the marriage of a couple who were engaged sixty years earlier but had broken up. Tom Susans and Judith Beston met at a teacher's training college in Brisbane in 1957 and fell in love. Tom bought a ring and proposed. But Judith's mother was adamantly opposed to the marriage, and that ended the relationship. Judith moved to New Zealand, took a teaching job, and eventually married someone else.

Tom, heartbroken, tried to find her. "She just disappeared," he said. "I didn't know where she was; I couldn't find her anywhere in Australia. I thought she was dead." He put the engagement ring and the wedding rings in a wooden cabinet, and he, too, married someone else.

Decades passed as Tom and Judith both married and raised families. But Tom went to every ten-year college reunion, still curious about Judith. She finally attended their fifty-year reunion, but there were four hundred people there, and Tom didn't see her. Only later did he learn she had showed up. Eventually he got her address, and for the next ten years they exchanged Christmas cards. After their spouses passed away, they began corresponding. Finally, Judith planned a trip to see Tom as part of her eightieth birthday celebration.

Tom, eighty-seven, wasted no time. He pulled out the box with the original rings and proposed again. She said yes straightaway, and the two were married in a small, emotional service. Judith marveled about "the chance of us meeting each other and the chances of us picking up where we left off."[12]

Our lives are ordered by the Lord, and He brings us together on earth in friendships, marriages, family units, relationships, and fellowship. The same God who brought us together the first time will reunite us, and we'll pick up where we left off—minus all disagreements and personality conflicts.

Shortly before he passed away from complications from pulmonary fibrosis in 2003, evangelist Bill Bright contemplated the nature of our heavenly experience. He wrote:

No reunion in history can even foreshadow what joy we will experience when we see loved ones and friends who went on before us. We are known. We are recognized (1 John 3:2). And we identify our loved ones, family, and friends. Brought together in the exquisite, all-surrounding presence of the Lord, our faces beam. Our countenances gleam, and we shout in such delight that angels glance at each other in wonderment: What full-throated, glad-hearted welcomes these blood-washed sinners give each other! How they adore the Lord Jesus! How they love Him! How they love each other![13]

Look Forward to a Risen Savior

And that brings us to the single greatest anticipation about heaven—our risen Savior. You will see Jesus Himself face to face. There's no more glorious verse in the Bible than Revelation 22:4: "They shall see His face."

This is your ultimate goal. This will be the single most phenomenal moment of your life. This is what you're living for, what you're waiting for, and what you're anticipating with all your heart. This is Celebration with a capital C—for Christ. You shall behold Him. As the blind poet Fanny Crosby proclaimed, "And I shall see Him face to face and tell the story saved by grace."[14]

The closer we get to heaven, the greater our longing for Jesus' face.

During the coronavirus pandemic, many families faced difficult separations. One South African, Matthew Kalil, was working in Iowa and found himself quarantined away from his wife, Clea, by nine thousand miles. Matthew eventually made it back to South Africa by taking a series of overnight flights. But when he arrived in Johannesburg, he was again quarantined. Finally he received permission to travel from Johannesburg to Cape Town. He was amazed at the emotions he felt.

"Interestingly," he wrote, "it was more difficult being away from my wife the closer I got to her. Like when I was in America, with the different time zones, it was easier. The closer I got the more I missed her."

The last hour of his journey home was tantalizing. "I was sharing my location via WhatsApp with Clea and so she knew when I was just around the block. She met me in the road and we just were both in tears. It really puts what is important into perspective."[15]

Kalil's journey sounds like a prototype for our own experience. The closer we get to heaven, the more we long to see our Lord and our loved ones. We should always be picking up forward momentum in life—constantly and eagerly accelerating onward "from glory to glory" (2 Cor. 3:18).

What do you think you'll be doing an hour after you die? Let me give you the answer to that from Scripture. You'll be doing the same thing you were doing an hour *before* you died—seeking to please Jesus in all you are and do. The Bible says, "So our aim is to please him always in everything we do, whether we are here in this body or away from this body and with him in heaven" (2 Cor. 5:9 TLB).

Your location may change, but not your core purpose in life. The things that pleased Christ on earth will please Him in heaven—and that means Christ-followers have an exhilarating celebration ahead that will make the heavens ring and the angels sing. When you get down to the last minute of your last hour of your last day on earth, you're ready for something more—something "far better" (Phil. 1:23). You're ready to go forward.

Go Forward with Jesus

Several years ago, Donna and I went to Tuscaloosa, Alabama, to speak at a prayer breakfast. I have been blessed with many opportunities to teach and preach the Bible, and when possible I accept the invitation. Sometimes I'm not even sure where I'm going. On this occasion, we drove to the hotel reserved for us, and I noticed it was near a huge stadium. Looking around, I realized we were on the campus of the University of Alabama on Paul W. Bryant Drive. I looked in my notes and saw that my speaking engagement was at the Bryant Conference Center.

When we arrived for the prayer breakfast, someone told me there was a man wanting to see me with a story to tell. His name was Red, and I could see why. He had long red hair, pulled back in a ponytail that went down the back of his neck. He looked like someone whose life had been hard.

He told me, "I tried everything to find some kind of peace here. I couldn't find it. My life was spiraling downhill, and just kept getting worse and worse. One day, I decided, 'That's it! I'm not going to do this anymore. I'm going to take my life.'

"I have driven to my work so often that I recalled a curve in the road. I began to think that if I went straight instead of bearing into the curve at, say, eighty miles an hour, I would hit a huge tree and it would be over for me. So I decided that would be the best way to take my own life.

"I got into my car, turned on my radio, found my rock-and-roll station, and turned it up, wide open, so I would have as much noise in the car as possible."

As he talked with me, I could visualize this man, sitting behind the wheel, intent on killing himself, and wanting some rock-and-roll music to distract him from the process. But for some reason, he told me, the radio acted up, which frustrated him so badly he finally took his fist and slammed it into the radio.

And—this is a true story!—our radio program, Turning Point, came on. Suddenly Red heard my voice as I was talking about heaven and about how to get there.

"It made me stop for a minute," Red told me. "I don't know what came over me, Pastor, but I shut my car off and then and there I prayed and received Christ as my Savior. And when I heard you were going to be here in Tuscaloosa I wanted to come and hug you and to tell you I'm going to heaven, and I'm so excited about it."

Like Red, you too can be excited about heaven. You can turn your forward into forever.

Don't miss the celebration and eternal joys of heaven! Jesus died and rose again to take you there, and He's gone ahead of you to get everything ready. The only way you can go forward is with Him. The whole human race is poisoned by sin, and the blood of Jesus is the only cure. He died on the cross for you, and the Bible says, "If you declare with your mouth, 'Jesus is Lord,' and believe in your heart that God raised him from the dead, you will be saved. For it is with your heart that you believe and are justified, and it is with your mouth that you profess your faith and are saved" (Rom. 10:9–10 NIV).

There's no going forward without Jesus!

And with Him, there's no turning back.

Acknowledgments

For fifty-seven years, my wife, Donna, and I have been going forward together. We have shared every dream, every detour, and every destination. This book sheds light on many of the spiritual principles that we have embraced. It should not surprise you to learn that, as we watch our oldest son, David, leading our organization by these principles, we are so very proud.

Walking alongside all of us on this journey is our administrative leader, Diane Sutherland, who for sixteen years has kept us all going forward. We write at least two books every year, and that would be impossible without Beau Sager directing the publication team. He works closely with Rob Morgan and Jennifer Hansen to make sure we hit our deadlines on time and communicate our message with clarity.

And when the last word is written and the book is released, look for Paul Joiner. He has been working overtime for many weeks to make sure we market our message and reach the maximum number of people. There is just no one like Paul Joiner, and we are blessed to have him on our team.

Finally, I want to pay tribute to my literary agent, Sealy Yates, and to our new W Publishing publisher, Damon Reiss. During a very difficult publishing season, you have never wavered in your confidence and belief in this book.

For all of the ways each of you have helped move this book forward, I want to express my profound gratitude.

On the front cover of this book is an arrow pointing forward. But all of us on this team want to together turn that arrow upward. Our goal is to glorify God and bring praise to His name!

—David Jeremiah
San Diego, California
July 2020

Notes

Introduction

1. Tommy Walker, "Song of the Week 2019–#4–'Forward,'" *Tommy Walker Ministries*, February 28, 2019, https://www.tommywalkerministries.org /media/song-of-the-week-2019-4-forward?rq=song%20of%20the%20 week.
2. Walker, "Song of the Week 2019."
3. F. B. Meyer, *Our Daily Walk* (Zeeland, MI: Reformed Church Publications, 2015), 181.

Chapter 1: Dream

1. Timothy S. Susanin, *Walt Before Mickey: Disney's Early Years, 1919–1928* (Jackson, MS: University Press of Mississippi, 2011), 180.
2. Henry Kaestner, William Norvell, Rusty Rueff, "Episode 90: 3-D Printing an Entire Village with Brett Hagler," *Faith Driven Entrpreneur*, accessed July 22, 2020, https://www.faithdrivenentrepreneur.org/podcast-inventory /2020/2/18/brett-hagler.
3. Joe Palca, "Alabama Woman Stuck in NYC Traffic in 1902 Invented the Windshield Wiper," *NPR*, July 25, 2017, https://www.npr. org/2017/07/25/536835744/alabama-woman-stuck-in-nyc-traffic-in-1902 -invented-the-windshield-wiper.
4. "11 Inspiring Quotes From WhatsApp's Billionaire Co-Founders," *Business Insider India*, February 21, 2014, https://www.businessinsider

.in/careers/11-inspiring-quotes-from-whatsapps-billionaire-co-founders
/slidelist/30806575.cms.

5. Parmy Olson, "Exclusive: The Rags-to-Riches Tale of How Jan Koum
   Built WhatsApp Into Facebook's New $19 Billion Baby," *Forbes*, February
   19, 2014, https://www.forbes.com/sites/parmyolson/2014/02/19/exclusive
   -inside-story-how-jan-koum-built-whatsapp-into-facebooks-new-19
   -billion-baby/#6f1955ea2fa1.

6. Dick Brogden, *Abiding Mission* (Eugene, OR: Wipf & Stock, 2016), 83.

7. Lindsay Elizabeth, "'They Got Joy, Heart, They Want to Work': Kentucky
   Pastor to Open Coffee Shop Staffed Entirely With Special Needs
   Employees," *Faithwire*, September 26, 2019, https://www.faithwire.com
   /2019/09/26/they-got-joy-heart-they-want-to-work-kentucky-pastor-to
   -open-coffee-shop-staffed-entirely-with-special-needs-employees/.

8. Brent Schlender, *Becoming Steve Jobs: The Evolution of a Reckless Upstart into
   a Visionary Leader* (New York, NY: Crown Publishing Group, 2016), 408.

9. Tim Hurson, *Think Better: An Innovator's Guide to Productive Thinking*
   (New York: McGraw-Hill, 2008), 104.

10. Dorothea Dix's story is told by Edith Deen in *Great Women of the
    Christian Faith* (Chappaqua, NY: Christian Herald Books, 1959), 367–70.

11. *Louis Braille Online Resource*, accessed May 4, 2020, https://www
    .louisbrailleonlineresource.org/.

Chapter 2: Pray

1. Catherine Marshall, *Adventures in Prayer* (Old Tappan, NJ: Revell, 1975),
   29–35.

2. Amanda Coers, "Bangs BBQ Business Sprung from Prayer Under a Pecan
   Tree," *Brownwood News*, May 15, 2017, https://brownwoodnews.com
   /bangs-bbq-business-sprung-from-prayer-under-a-pecan-tree/.

3. Caleb Parke, "WWII Veteran and Pastor, 95, Gets More than 180K
   Praying for Revival," *Fox News*, May 4, 2020, https://www.foxnews.com
   /us/revival-prayer-event-north-carolina-veteran-pastor-coronavirus
   -update.

4. E. M. Bounds, *The Complete Works of E. M. Bounds on Prayer* (Grand
   Rapids, MI: Baker, 1990), 153, 162.

5. Mark Cole, "God Answered My Prayer for a Wife . . . (and Much More),"
   Following God: The Grand Adventure, May 15, 2014, http://www
   .markcole.ca/god-answered-my-prayer-for-a-wifeand-much-more/.

6. Jim George, *Knowing God Through Prayer* (Eugene, OR: Harvest House, 2005), 98.

7. Brenda Poe, "9/11 Survivor: God Answered My Prayer," *Santa Maria Times*, January 20, 2002, https://santamariatimes.com/news/local /survivor-god-answered-my-prayer/article_25fa2e5c-ff52–5552-b647 -c227a8d35e7f.html.

8. Susie Larson, *Your Powerful Prayers* (Minneapolis, MN: Bethany House, 2016), 153–59.

9. Karen Rhea, "The Mule: A Missionary Story," *Just Between Us*, accessed May 14, 2020, https://justbetweenus.org/faith/the-mule-a-missionary -rescue-story/.

10. Henry A. Buttz, "Is Prayer a Lost Art?" *The Homiletic Review 55* (January to June, 1908): 419.

11. George Muller, "Joy of Answered Prayer," *George Muller.org*, August 23, 2015, https://www.georgemuller.org/quotes/joy-of-answered-prayer.

12. Dionna Sanchez, "Celebrating the Joy of Answered Prayer," *Beauty in the Storm*, November 3, 2014, https://www.beautyinthestorm.com/2014/11 /celebrating-joy-of-answered-prayer.html.

13. Catherine Marshall, *Adventures in Prayer* (Old Tappan, NJ: Revell, 1975), 39.

Chapter 3: Choose

1. Virginia Kelly, "His Parachute Got Stuck on the Plane's Wheel and He Was Suspended in Midair with Little Chance of Survival—then Another Plane Came to Rescue," *Reader's Digest*, February 20, 2020, https://www .rd.com/true-stories/survival/miracle-in-midair/.

2. Brian Duffy, "Return to Sender; It's a Mail Mix Up as Twinsburg Couple Gets 55,000 Pieces of Mail," *19 News*, February 1, 2020, https://www. cleveland19.com/2020/02/01/return-sender-its-mail-mix-up-twinsburg -couple-gets-pieces-mail/.

3. Greg McKeown, *Essentialism: The Disciplined Pursuit of Less* (New York: Crown, 2014), 16.

4. Will Maurle, "Chris Pratt Sets Incredible Example at Teen Choice Awards: 'I Love God and You Should Too,'" *CBN News*, August 13, 2018, https:// www1.cbn.com/cbnnews/2018/august/chris-pratt-sets-incredible-example -at-teen-choice-awards-lsquo-i-love-god-and-you-should-too-rsquo.

5. Rod Culbertson, *Do I Love God* (Eugene, OR: Wipf & Stock, 2017), xv, 4.

6. Elisabeth Elliot, *Through Gates of Spendor* (Lincoln, NE: Back to the Bible Broadcast, 1981), 50–51.

7. Michael Ashcraft, "Jesus Movement Among Cops Only Hope for Excessive Domestic Abuse, Divorce and Alcoholism in Their Ranks," *God Reports*, February 19, 2020, http://godreports.com/2020/02/jesus -movement-among-cops-only-hope-for-excessive-domestic-abuse -divorce-and-alcoholism-in-their-ranks/.

8. Brad Hall, "Preparing for a Nursery Has Taught Me About Priorities," *Times Tribune,* February 23, 2020, https://www.thetimestribune.com /opinion/columns/preparing-for-a-nursery-has-taught-me-about- priorities/article_f8ea7f3a-da34–5013–88d3-b372bee55992.html.

9. Jesse Green, "Is Broadway Stuck on Replay," *New York Times,* February 24, 2020, https://www.nytimes.com/2020/02/24/theater/revivals -broadway.html.

10. See James Clear, "Warren Buffett's '2 List' Strategy: How to Maximize Your Focus and Master Your Priorities," *James Clear,* accessed June 23, 2020, https://jamesclear.com/buffett-focus.

11. McKeown, *Essentialism*, 9–10.

12. Maritza Manresa, *Learning to Say NO! When You Usually Say Yes* (Ocala, FL: Atlantic Publishing Group, 2012), 56–60.

13. Adapted from David Jeremiah, *Prayer the Great Adventure* (Sisters, OR: Multnomah Publishers, Inc., 1997), 107–108.

14. Kelly, "His Parachute Got Stuck on the Plane's Wheel."

Chapter 4: Focus

1. Luciano Pavarotti, "Guideposts Classics: Luciano Pavarotti on Making the Most of God's Gifts," *Guideposts*, October 11, 2017, https://www .guideposts.org/better-living/entertainment/music/guideposts-classics -luciano-pavarotti-on-making-the-most-of-gods.

2. Jason Duaine Hahn, "Oldest Living Man Celebrates 112th Birthday amid Social Distancing in UK: 'It Is Bizarre,'" *People*, March 31, 2020, https:// people.com/human-interest/oldest-living-man-honored-quarantine-uk/.

3. Madi Turpin, "IWU Pastor Faces Grim Diagnosis," *The Echo*, March 9, 2020, https://www.theechonews.com/article/2020/03/iwu-pastor-faces -grim-diagnosis.

4. Bill Sorrell, "It's Worth the Hustle," *Word & Way*, January 23, 2020, https://wordandway.org/2020/01/23/its-worth-the-hustle/.

5. Kevin Porter, "Rick Warren: Becoming More Like Jesus Takes a Lifetime of Spiritual Growth," *Christian Post*, January 19, 2017, https://www .christianpost.com/news/rick-warren-becoming-like-jesus-takes-lifetime -spiritual-growth.html.

6. Michael McGowan, "How Roger Bannister and Australian John Landy Raced to Break the Four-Minute Mile," *The Guardian*, March 5, 2018, https://www.theguardian.com/sport/2018/mar/05/how-roger-bannister -and-australian-john-landy-raced-to-break-the-four-minute-mile.

7. N. T. Wright, *Paul: A Biography* (New York: HarperOne, 2018), 2.

8. G. Walter Hansen, *The Letter to the Philippians* (Grand Rapids, MI: Eerdmans, 2009), 252.

9. William E. Barton, *The Life of Clara Barton*, accessed June 24, 2020, https://archive.org/stream/LifeOfClaraBartonFounderOfTheAmerican RedCrossV.2/LifeOfClaraBarton_v2_Barton71043756_djvu.txt.

10. Harry J. Kazianis, "I Was Bullied as a Kid. It Almost Ruined My Adult Life," *The Week*, June 20, 2017, https://theweek.com/articles/703696 /bullied-kid-almost-ruined-adult-life.

11. Tony Bombacino, "Speical Needs Dad: The Role that Nothing (and Everything) Prepared Me For," *Real Food Blends*, December 9, 2015, https://www.realfoodblends.com/special-needs-dad-the-role-that -everything-and-nothing-prepared-me-for/.

12. Adapted from David Jeremiah, *Count It All Joy* (Colorado Springs, CO: David C. Cook, 2016), 175.

13. Adapted from Ronald Miller, "Florence Chadwick—an Inspirational Story," accessed March 4, 2020, https://ronaldfmiller44.blogspot.com /2013/04/florence-chadwickan-inspirational-story.html. See also Randy Alcorn, "Florence Chadwick and the Fog," *Eternal Perspective Ministries*, January 21, 2020, https://www.epm.org/resources/2010/Jan/21/florence -chadwick-and-fog/.

14. Adapted from Gary Keller with Jay Papasan, *One Thing* (Austin, TX: Bard Press, 2012), 21. See also *Gilbert Tuhabonye*, https://gilberttuhabonye.com/.

15. R. Kent Hughes, *1–2 Timothy and Titus* (Wheaton, IL: Crossway, 2012), 211.

Chapter 5: Risk

1. Jean Hanson, "Worry and Fear Kept Me From Taking Action: What I Did to Move Forward," *The Janitorial Store*, accessed June 24, 2020, https://www

.thejanitorialstore.com/public/Worry-and-Fear-Kept-Me-From-Taking -Action-2165.cfm.

2. Erwin Raphael McManus, *Seizing Your Divine Moment* (Nashville, TN: Thomas Nelson, 1982), 147.

3. John Tierney and Roy F. Baumeister, *The Power of Bad: How the Negativity Effect Rules Us, and How We Can Rule It* (New York: Penguin, 2019), 11–12.

4. Hanson, "Worry and Fear Kept Me From Taking Action."

5. Story told by Michael Hyatt, *Your Best Year Ever* (Grand Rapids, MI: Baker Books, 2018) 193–94.

6. Bruce R. Miller, "Geena Davis Remembers Her Olympic Run, Classic Films," *Sioux City Journal*, August 14, 2016, https://siouxcityjournal.com /entertainment/television/geena-davis-remembers-her-olympic-run -classic-films/article_31297ad8-f64b-50f7-a4c2-c9679345a09a.html.

7. Kay Redfield Jamison, *Exuberance: The Passion for Life* (New York: Vintage Books, 2004), 4.

8. Jessica Long, "Fight for the Fatherless," accessed May 4, 2020, https:// fightforthefatherless.org/jessica-long.

9. Doug Bean, "She's Come This Far By Faith: The Unstoppable Jessica Long," *Celebrate Life*, July–August 2014, https://clmagazine.org/topic /human-dignity/shes-come-this-far-by-faith-the-unstoppable -jessica-long/.

10. Quoted by Norman Vincent Peale in *Enthusiasm Makes the Difference* (Englewood Cliffs, NJ: Prentice-Hall, 1967), 4.

11. Robert Beatty, "Age No Obstacle for 71-Year-Old Designer," *South Florida Times*, November 18, 2010, https://www.sfltimes.com/uncategorized/age -no-obstacle-for-71-year-old-designer.

Chapter 6: Pursue

1. "Pop Star, Had It All, Felt Empty and This Happened," *Authors-choice*, November 25, 2019, https://authorschoice.org/2019/11/25/pop-star-had-it -all-felt-empty-and-this-happened/.

2. Tom Hamilton, "Is Joseph Schooling Ready for More Gold After Being the Last Man to Beat Michael Phelps?" *ESPN*, March 30, 2020, https://www .espn.com/olympics/story/_/id/28922185/is-joseph-schooling-last-man -beat-michael-phelps-ready-more-gold.

3. Will Maule, "Manny Pacquiao: 'My Life Was Empty Until I Met Jesus,'"

Hello Christian, October 4, 2016, https://hellochristian.com/4720-manny
-pacquiao-my-life-was-empty-until-i-met-jesus.

4. Eros Villanueva, "Manny Pacquiao Tests Negative for Coronavirus,"
   ESPN, March 27, 2020, https://www.espn.com/boxing/story/_/id/28964912
   /manny-pacquiao-tests-negative-coronavirus.

5. Wendy Rhodes, "Rick Allen, Def Leppard's One-Armed Drummer, Also
   Tries Hand at Painting," *Broward Palm Beach New Times*, January 10,
   2020, https://www.browardpalmbeach.com/music/rick-allen-def-leppards
   -one-armed-drummer-also-tries-hand-at-painting-10465440.

6. E. E. Cummings, *A Miscellany* (New York: Liverlight, 1986), 363.

7. Nathan Foster, "Michael Lee '90 Runs His Race," *Azusa Pacific
   University*, March 23, 2020, https://www.apu.edu/articles/michael
   -lee-90-runs-his-race/.

8. Natalie Stevens, "Oswego Resident Changing Lives One Tattoo at a Time,"
   Patch, December 19, 2012, https://patch.com/illinois/oswego/oswego
   -resident-ink-180-tattoo-sex-trafficking-gang-t0fe40da180.

9. "The Ink 180 Story," *Ink180*, accessed April 23, 2020, http://ink180.com
   /the-ink180-story/.

10. Karen Mahoney, "To Protect and Serve: Bible Church's New Pastor Comes
    from Police Force to God's Force," *Kenosha News*, January 31, 2020,
    https://www.kenoshanews.com/lifestyles/faith-and-values/to-protect
    -and-serve-bible-church-s-new-pastor-comes/article_02a816f4–1216
    –5968-b1d2–777532a1f50f.html.

11. Eddie Jones, "Calling Down the Light," *CBN*, accessed April 23, 2020,
    https://www1.cbn.com/devotions/calling-down-light.

12. Quoted in Randy Bishop, "Just Give Me Jesus," *Today's Christian Woman*,
    accessed May 7, 2020, https://www.todayschristianwoman.com/articles
    /2000/september/just-give-me-jesus.html?start=6.

13. Alex Sibley, "Horsewoman Finds True Joy in Jesus," *Southwestern Baptist
    Theological Seminary*, October 26, 2018, https://swbts.edu/news/everyday-
    evangelism/horsewoman-finds-true-joy-jesus/.

14. Abba Eban, *Abba Eban: An Autobiography* (New York: Random House:
    1977), 609.

15. Jon Krakauer, *Into Thin Air* (New York: Doubleday/Anchor Books, 1997),
    3–4.

16. Mrs. Howard Taylor, *Borden of Yale '09* (London: The China Inland
    Mission, 1926), 260.

Chapter 7: Believe

1. Mark Schlabach, "Dabo Swinney Overcame Pain and Poverty to Be on the Cusp of History," *ESPN*, January 6, 2016, https://www.espn.com /college-football/story/_/id/14519758/dabo-swinney-overcame-pain -poverty-reach-new-heights-clemson.
2. Jon Gordon, *The Power of Positive Leadership* (Hoboken, NJ: John Wiley & Sons, 2017), 63.
3. John Henry Jowett, "Apostolic Optimism," *Bible Hub*, accessed May 21, 2020, https://biblehub.com/sermons/auth/various/apostolic_optimism .htm.
4. Travis Bradberry, "Why the Best Leaders Have Conviction," *Forbes*, June 28, 2016, https://www.forbes.com/sites/travisbradberry/2016/06/28 /why-the-best-leaders-have-conviction/#7a8ce97f1c8d.
5. Alison Bonaguro, "Carrie Underwood Considers God's Unconditional Love," *CMT News*, December 23, 2013, http://www.cmt.com/news /1719548/carrie-underwood-considers-gods-unconditional-love/.
6. John Stott, *Romans: God's Good News for the World* (Downers Grove, IL: InterVarsity Press, 1994), 259.
7. Stephanie Nolasco, "'Little House on the Prairie' Actress Wendi Lou Lee Says She Relied on God to Help Her Face Her Brain Tumor," *Fox News*, September 13, 2019, https://www.foxnews.com/entertainment/little -house-on-the-prairie-wendi-lou-lee.
8. Brennan Manning, *The Wisdom of Tenderness* (New York: HarperCollins, 2002), 25–26.
9. Jennice Vilhauer, *Think Forward to Thrive* (Novato, CA: New World Library, 2014), 1.
10. Dick Van Dyke, *Keep Moving* (New York: Weinstein Books, 2015), ix–xi.
11. H. Norman Wright, *A Better Way to Think* (Grand Rapids, MI: Baker 2011), 11–18.
12. Joseph Telushkin, *Words That Hurt, Words That Heal* (New York: HarperCollins, 2019), 3.
13. Leslie D. Weatherhead, *Prescription for Anxiety* (New York: Abingdon), 21–22.
14. Adapted from Dennis N. T. Perkins, *Leading at the Edge* (New York: American Management Association, 2000), 74–75.
15. Linda C. DeFew, "No More Excuses" in *Chicken Soup for the Soul: The Power of Positive*, ed. by Jack Canfield, Mark Victor Hansen, and Amy

Newmark (Cos Cob, CT: Chicken Soup for the Soul Publishing, nd),
Kindle location 368–407.

16. Martin E. P. Seligman, *Learned Optimism* (New York: Alfred A. Knopf,
1990), 4–5.

17. "Grin and Bear It! Smiling Facilitates Stress Recovery," *Association for
Psychological Science*, July 30, 2012, https://www.psychologicalscience.org
/news/releases/smiling-facilitates-stress-recovery.html.

18. John Mason, *Believe You Can* (Grand Rapids, MI: Revell, 2004), 144–46.

Chapter 8: Invest

1. Doug Bender, "How to Lose Everything and Find Peace," *Faith Gateway*,
December 12, 2019, https://www.faithgateway.com/how-to-lose
-everything-and-find-peace/#.XnUOttNKjUI.

2. Tammy La Gorce, "Retired, or Hoping to Be, and Saddled with Student
Loans," *New York Times*, February 28, 2020, https://www.nytimes.com
/2020/02/26/business/retirement-student-loan-debt.html.

3. Ross McCall, "When You Don't Like Reading the Bible," *Cru*, accessed
June 25, 2020, https://www.cru.org/car/en/blog/share-the-gospel
/obstacles-to-faith/when-you-dont-like-reading-the-bible.html.

4. Valerie Hildebeitel, "Murphy the Surf Brings Jesus to Jail," *The Morning
Call*, May 15, 1988, https://www.mcall.com/news/mc-xpm-1988–05–15
–2630408-story.html.

5. Daniel P. Kinkade, "A Series of Left Turns," *The Gideon's International*,
January 10, 2020, https://www.gideons.org/blog/A_Series_of_Left_Turns.

6. Patrick M. Morley, "How to Develop a Personal Ministry," *Man in the
Mirror*, December 10, 2008, https://maninthemirror.org/2008/12/10/13
how-to-develop-a-personal-ministry/.

7. Sue Staughn, "Meet Mr. Bill, the Bike Man," *ABC 3 WEAR TV*, January 21,
2019, https://weartv.com/features/angels-in-our-midst/meet-mr-bill-the
-bike-man.

8. Cathy Free, "Former Texas Pastor Opens Free Auto Shop for Women Who
Are 'Short on Money and Long on Car Troubles,'" *People*, September 28,
2017, https://people.com/human-interest/former-texas-pastor-free-auto
-shop-gods-garage/.

9. Trudy Smith, "Why I Go To Church Even When I Don't Feel Like It,"
Relevant, June 6, 2016, https://relevantmagazine.com/god/why-i-go
-church-even-when-i-dont-feel-it/.

10. Randy Alcorn, *Money, Possessions, and Eternity* (Carol Stream, IL: Tyndale House Publishers, Inc., 2003), 96.

11. Clint Morgan, "Stewardship Lesson," *One Magazine*, March 2018, 7.

12. Ralph Barton Perry, *The Thought and Character of William James* (London: Oxford University Press, 1935), 289.

13. Tony Evans, *What Matters Most* (Chicago, IL: Moody Press, 1997), 352.

Chapter 9: Finish

1. Jay Levin, "No Argument Here: 94-Year-Old Attorney Is a Marvel," *North Jersey*, March 13, 2017, https://www.northjersey.com/story/news/2017/03/13/no-argument-here-94-year-old-attorney-marvel/97264910/.

2. Jon Acuff, *Finish: Give Yourself the Gift of Done* (New York: Penguin Random House, 2018), 2.

3. Jefferson Smith, "63% of Your Readers Don't Finish Your Book. Here's Why," *Creativity Hacker*, August 18, 2015, https://creativityhacker.ca/2015/08/18/63-percent-of-readers/.

4. Adapted from Scott Thomas, "Pastors Who Finish Well," *Acts 29*, November 14, 2008, https://www.acts29.com/pastors-who-finish-well/.

5. Harry Bollback, *Our Incredible Journey Home* (Schroon Lake, NY: Word of Life Fellowship, 2019), 6–7, 13.

6. Kiara, "Retired and Lonely," *Retirement-Online Community*, accessed February 3, 2020, https://www.retirement-online.com/retired-lonely.html.

7. Bob Buford, *Finishing Well* (Brentwood, TN: Integrity Publishers, 2004), 247.

8. Ibid., 124–125.

9. David Asman and Adam Meyerson, *The Wall Street Journal on Management: The Best of the Manager's Journal* (New York: New American Library, 1986), 7.

10. J. Oswald Sanders, *Enjoying Your Best Years: Staying Young While Growing Older* (Grand Rapids, MI: Discovery House Publishers, 1993), 66.

Chapter 10: Celebrate

1. "Millionaire Lottery Winner Goes Back to Job at McDonald's . . . Because He Misses His Workmates," *Evening Standard*, March 25, 2008, https://www.standard.co.uk/news/millionaire-lottery-winner-goes-back-to-job-at-mcdonalds-because-he-misses-his-workmates-6688295.html.

2. Ange Shepard, "Living the Dream" in *Chicken Soup for the Soul: The*

Power of Positive, ed. by Jack Canfield, Mark Victor Hansen, and Amy Newmark (Cos Cob, CT: Chicken Soup for the Soul Publishing, 2012), 223–225.

3. C. S. Lewis, *Mere Christianity* (New York: Macmillan, 1980), 119.
4. Kara Sutyak, "Howland Boy Bravely Battling Leukemia Gets Wonderful Welcome Back to School," *Fox 8*, April 9, 2019, https://fox8.com/news /video-howland-boy-bravely-battling-leukemia-gets-wonderful-welcome -back-to-school/.
5. Michelle Regna, "Michael Bublé Surprised His Grandpa's Caretaker With a Renovation," *HGTV*, May 4, 2020, https://www.hgtv.com/shows /celebrity-iou/michael-buble-renovation-pictures.
6. Joni Eareckson Tada, *Heaven: Your Real Home* (Grand Rapids, MI: Zondervan, 1995), 14.
7. David Jeremiah, *The Book of Signs* (Nashville, TN: W Publishing, 2019), 194.
8. Julia Czerwonatis and Peter de Graaf, "Queen's Birthday Honours: Seven of Northland's Finest Recognised," *The Northland Age*, June 1, 2020, https://www.nzherald.co.nz/northland-age/news/article.cfm?c_id =1503402&objectid=12335420.
9. John Peck, *John Peck: Marine, Author, Speaker & Survivor,* accessed June 16, 2020, https://www.johnpeckjourney.com/.
10. Randy Alcorn, *Heaven* (Carol Stream, IL: Tyndale House Publishers, Inc., 2004), 396.
11. Dr. Vernon M. Whaley, *Exalt His Name* (Calumet City, IL: Evangelical Training Association, 2017), 23–24.
12. Inga Stünzner, "Couple Has Second Chance at Love, Tying the Knot 60 Years After Their First Engagement," *ABC News*, October 18, 2019, https://www.abc.net.au/news/2019–10–19/second-chance-at-love-60-years -on/11614886.
13. Bill Bright, *The Journey Home* (Nashville, TN: Thomas Nelson, 2003), 155.
14. Fanny Crosby, "Saved by Grace," 1891.
15. Murray Williams, "From the US to Home: Husband's Long Repatriation Journey Ends with Teary Reunion," *News 24*, May 24, 2020, https://www .news24.com/news24/southafrica/news/watch-from-the-us-to-home -husbands-long-repatriation-journey-ends-with-teary-reunion-20200524.

Scripture Index

Index

Index

About the Author

Dr. David Jeremiah is the founder of Turning Point, an international ministry committed to providing Christians with sound Bible teaching through radio and television, the Internet, live events, and resource materials and books. He is the author of more than fifty books, including *Everything You Need, Is This the End?, The Spiritual Warfare Answer Book, David Jeremiah Morning and Evening Devotions, Airship Genesis Kids Study Bible,* and *The Jeremiah Study Bible.*

Dr. Jeremiah serves as the senior pastor of Shadow Mountain Community Church in San Diego, California, where he resides with his wife, Donna. They have four grown children and twelve grandchildren.

stay connected to the teaching of

DR. DAVID JEREMIAH

· · · · · · · ·

Publishing | Radio | Television | Online

FURTHER YOUR STUDY OF THIS BOOK

• • • • • • • •

Forward Resource Materials

To enhance your study on this important topic, we recommend the correlating audio message album, study guide, and DVD messages from the *Forward* series.

Audio Message Album

The material found in this book originated from messages presented by Dr. Jeremiah at Shadow Mountain Community Church where he serves as senior pastor. These ten messages are conveniently packaged in an accessible audio album.

Study Guide

This 144-page study guide correlates with the messages from the *Forward* series by Dr. Jeremiah. Each lesson provides an outline, an overview, and group and personal application questions for each topic.

DVD Message Presentations

Watch Dr. Jeremiah deliver the *Forward* original messages in this special DVD collection.

To order these products, call us at 1-800-947-1993
or visit us online at www.DavidJeremiah.org.

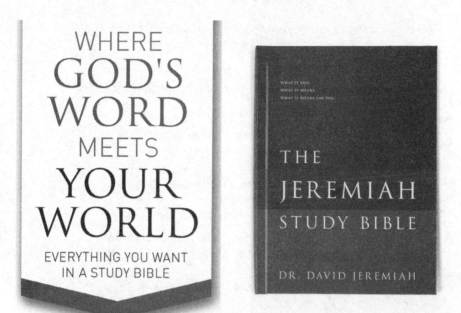

Additional resources

· · · · · · · ·

Take advantage of three great ways to let Dr. David Jeremiah
give you spiritual direction every day!

Turning Points Magazine and Devotional

Receive Dr. Jeremiah's magazine,
Turning Points, each month:
- Thematic study focus
- 48 pages of life-changing reading
- Relevant articles
- Daily devotional readings and more!

Request *Turning Points* magazine today!
(800) 947-1993 | <u>DavidJeremiah.org/Magazine</u>

Daily Turning Point E-Devotional

Receive a daily e-devotion from Dr. Jeremiah
that will strengthen your walk with God and
encourage you to live the authentic Christian life.

Sign up for your free e-devotional today!
<u>www.DavidJeremiah.org/Devo</u>

Turning Point Mobile App

Access Dr. Jeremiah's video teachings,
audio sermons, and more . . . whenever and
wherever you are!

Download your free app today!
<u>www.DavidJeremiah.org/App</u>

BOOKS WRITTEN BY DAVID JEREMIAH

• • • • • • • • •

- Escape the Coming Night
- Count It All Joy
- The Handwriting on the Wall
- Invasion of Other Gods
- Angels—Who They Are and How They

  Help…What the Bible Reveals
- The Joy of Encouragement
- Prayer—The Great Adventure
- Overcoming Loneliness
- God in You
- Until Christ Returns
- Stories of Hope
- Slaying the Giants in Your Life
- My Heart's Desire
- Sanctuary
- The Things That Matter
- The Prayer Matrix
- 31 Days to Happiness—Searching for

  Heaven on Earth
- When Your World Falls Apart
- Turning Points
- Discover Paradise

- Captured by Grace
- Grace Givers
- Why the Nativity?
- Signs of Life
- Life-Changing Moments with God
- Hopeful Parenting
- 1 Minute a Day—Instant Inspiration for

  the Busy Life
- Grandparenting—Faith That Survives

  Generations
- In the Words of David Jeremiah
- What in the World Is Going On?
- The Sovereign and the Suffering
- The 12 Ways of Christmas
- What to Do When You Don't Know

  What to Do
- Living with Confidence in a Chaotic

  World
- The Coming Economic Armageddon
- Pathways, Your Daily Walk with God
- What the Bible Says About Love,

  Marriage, and Sex

To order these books, call us at 1-800-947-1993 or
visit us online at www.DavidJeremiah.org.

BOOKS WRITTEN BY DAVID JEREMIAH

• • • • • • • • •

- I Never Thought I'd See the Day

- Journey, Your Daily Adventure with God

- The Unchanging Word of God

- God Loves You: He Always Has–He Always Will

- Discovery, Experiencing God's Word Day by Day

- What Are You Afraid Of?

- Destination, Your Journey with God

- Answers to Questions About Heaven

- Answers to Questions About Spiritual Warfare

- Answers to Questions About Adversity

- Answers to Questions About Prophecy

- Quest—Seeking God Daily

- The Upward Call

- Ten Questions Christians are Asking

- Understanding the 66 Books of the Bible

- A.D.—The Revolution That Changed the World

- Agents of the Apocalypse

- Agents of Babylon

- Reset—Ten Steps to Spiritual Renewal

- People Are Asking … Is This the End?

- Hope for Today

- Hope—An Anchor for Life

- 30 Days of Prayer

- Revealing the Mysteries of Heaven

- Greater Purpose

- The God You May Not Know

- Overcomer: 8 Ways to Live a Life of Unstoppable Strength, Unmovable Faith, and Unbelievable Power

- In Moments Like These

- The Book of Signs—31 Undeniable Prophecies of the Apocalypse

- Everything You Need: 8 Essential Steps to a Life of Confidence in the Promises of God

- Daily in His Presence

- Answers to Questions About Living in the Last Days

- The Jesus You May Not Know

- Shelter in God

To order these books, call us at 1-800-947-1993 or visit us online at www.DavidJeremiah.org.